# MORE THAN A STORY

# More
# Than a Story

## ELLEN E. LARSON
## DAVID V. ESTERLINE

**VICTOR BOOKS**®

A DIVISION OF SCRIPTURE PRESS PUBLICATIONS INC.
USA CANADA ENGLAND

*St. Mark's Church*
*Highland, MD 20777*

Cover design © 1990 Courtesy of and Supplied by John Kaldor

Scripture quotations are from the *Holy Bible, New International Version,* © 1973, 1978, 1984, International Bible Society. Used by permission of Zondervan Bible Publishers.

Recommended Dewey Decimal Classification: 226.8
Suggested Subject Heading: BIBLE, N.T., PARABLES OF JESUS

Library of Congress Catalog Card Number: 91-65451
ISBN: 0-89693-813-1

1 2 3 4 5 6 7 8 9 10 Printing/Year 95 94 93 92 91

VICTOR BOOKS
A division of SP Publications, Inc.
Wheaton, Illinois 60187

# CONTENTS

# INTRODUCTION

You are holding in your hands a most useful guide to studying the parables of Jesus. Whether you need help seeing afresh what the Bible is saying, or need help thinking of ways to apply the truths you learn, or need the structure and motivation that a study guide can give, you will benefit from using this book.

Each session in the guide has four components: inductive study questions to walk you through the Scriptures; a narrative section giving more background information; exercises and challenges to apply Bible truth to your own life; and a leader's guide to aid in group study. Whether you study alone or lead a group, you may choose those questions or exercises that fit your needs or your group's.

If you are studying on your own, make a point of sharing what you are learning with someone else. You will solidify lessons in your mind while you bless your friend.

If you are part of a group, you will find it most helpful to work through the study questions on your own before the group meets. Then you will be ready to share what you learned from the passage and how it applies to your life, plus any questions that arose as you studied. Members will profit from hearing one another's insights and perceptions.

Using the study questions, work through the Scripture passage *before* you read the narrative section; in this way, your initial findings will all be original.

Throughout the study, remember that the Holy Spirit is your teacher. Ask Him to give you eyes to see His truth and a heart ready to obey it.

As you come across questions that call for you to connect the truth of the passage to your own life, answer them prayerfully. Let the

Spirit guide you in applying God's Word to your life. When you find something in the passage that makes you feel grateful to God, thank Him! When something leads you to praise Him, stop and do so! When the Spirit points to something in your life that doesn't measure up to what you're reading in Scripture, let Him speak to you. Confess any sin and allow God to cleanse you and lead you in the right direction.

To be properly equipped for each study, you will need a Bible, this study guide, plus any other materials named by the leader (if you have one). You may want to have a notebook in which to record your thoughts and discoveries from your personal study and group meetings. You could also use it to list prayer requests in a group setting plus their resolutions.

# 1

# WHAT, WHY, AND HOW
*Introduction to Parables*

## LEARNING THE STORY

A study of the parables must begin with the parables themselves. If possible, read straight through the first three Gospels—Matthew, Mark, and Luke—and list each parable as you come to it. Virtually all the parables of Jesus (which number between 30 and 60, depending on one's exact definition) are found in these three Gospels. This straight-through reading will be extremely helpful for placing the parables in their literary settings and seeing the range of their content and complexity. If you cannot now read through the complete Gospels of Matthew, Mark, and Luke, focus on those chapters where the majority of the parables appear: Matthew 13; 18; 20–25; Mark 4; 12–13; and Luke 10; 12–20.

Read several parables and answer the following questions.
1. What do you think a parable is? After answering, see the dictionary definition.


2. What are the parables about? Look first at the outward details—the characters in the story, the setting, the event, and the emotions portrayed. How do they compare across the range of parables? How can these parables give you a greater understanding of the kingdom of God?


3. Why did Jesus use parables?


4. If Jesus lived in our time and place and used settings well known

to us in His parables, what characters and events would He use?

5. What are some examples of Jesus' teachings that are not parables?

6. How does a parable compare with an allegory, a fable, a morality tale, or a folk tale?

7. Why should we take the time to study the parables today?

# LOOKING BEHIND THE STORY

The parables are the bedrock of the teachings of Jesus. They make up about one third of His recorded teaching, providing vibrant, intriguing pictures of life in Jesus' time and leading us straight to the heart of His urgent message of the coming kingdom of God.

**What Exactly *Is* a Parable?**
The old Sunday School definition, "An earthly story with a heavenly meaning," is not far off. A parable is a comparison using an illustration from everyday life or from nature to point to some spiritual truth and to elicit a response.

The Greek word *parabole* (meaning "comparison" or "analogy"—the most basic meaning being "to throw something alongside something else") is wider in meaning than the parable, as it includes riddles, proverbs, and wise sayings, as well as the short stories we think of as parables. The background for Jesus' parables is found in His Jewish heritage. In the Old Testament, "parable" refers to any verbal image, from any short and simple metaphor to the detailed and famous story told by Nathan the prophet (2 Sam. 12:1-4). A parable, then, is a comparison which may be short ("Be as shrewd as snakes" [Matt. 10:16], though some would call this a simile and say that it is too short to be a true parable) or as long and complex as the Parable of the Lost Son in Luke 15. In fact, most of us use parables in some form all the time, from something as simple as calling our children pumpkins to giving an involved explanation to convince others.

## Why Did Jesus Teach in Parables?

While they are certainly interesting, sometimes entertaining, and often sharp and penetrating, the parables are not necessarily easy to understand. They are much more than mere illustrations, more than stories meant to make a certain meaning simple to understand or easier to swallow.

It is clear from the New Testament, especially the three Gospels where we find the parables, that Jesus' clear-cut goal was to announce the great good news of the coming of the kingdom of God. The time had come; it was now possible to enter and live under the reign of God. For such important and wonderful news, we would expect to hear dramatic proclamations. Instead, Jesus tells stories about ordinary people.

As any teacher knows, if you want to teach what is not understood, you must begin with what *is* understood. The parables are examples of this simple approach; they begin with elements and experiences from the world of the hearers.

Parables demand listeners' attention. Who can resist such word pictures, such compelling short stories? Jesus put His truth into story form to be certain of His hearers' attention. With most people, a good story is the first thing to draw their attention. Without that interest, they will neither listen to nor retain what is being taught.

Parables make abstract truths concrete. In His parables, Jesus puts the great ideas of time and salvation into pictures and stories. With the stories in this study, we are drawn to discover the truth for ourselves and to remember it. The teacher knows that the best teaching is that which leads learners to uncover meanings for themselves. Lessons taught externally (given by lecture or meant to be copied down and memorized) tend to be forgotten quickly. But when learners must draw their own conclusions from their own thinking, the lesson becomes part of life and is easier to remember. The parables present us with stories and then the challenge: *So, what does the parable mean? Why did Jesus tell it? What is the meaning in the story* for us?

To begin with, Jesus told parables to catch the attention of His hearers and to present the crux of His message in a vivid, living, and memorable way. The parable is a challenge—a challenge to the hearer to work out its meaning, a challenge to think.

On another side, Jesus told stories about women and men rather than teaching in precepts because He is actively concerned about real women and men. For Him, it's people first—not ideas. That Jesus thought ordinary people and ordinary life could be used as instructive comparisons for the kingdom of God seems remarkable. This fact tells us about the kind of person Jesus was: not some academic theologian of stern demeanor and abstract theories, but someone able to talk to and reach ordinary people. The parables show Jesus immersed in the world He lived in, involved in the successes and failures of individuals and their families, farms, businesses, and politics.

We must add, of course, that Jesus taught even more profoundly by His actions, by the way He conducted His whole life. The center of the Good News He proclaimed is the forgiveness that is available to everyone; and how could this be more forcefully illustrated than by Jesus' table fellowship with the outcasts of society? An invitation to eat with someone was, in His day, a strong sign of acceptance, an offer of peace and trust. Jesus associated again and again with ordinary persons — and even the hated tax collectors and prostitutes.

**How Do We Study the Parables?**
It is important to recognize, first of all, the distance that separates us from Jesus and the parables. The distance in time is obvious; but we need to notice also the political and religious distance, to say nothing of the distance of everyday life. How many of us know from experience what would happen if we put new wine into old wineskins?

Remember that Jesus *spoke* the parables. The parables were not first read, pondered over with thick commentaries, discussed at length, explored in seminars, all in the hope of eventual interpretation. Rather, as people listened, they had flashes of understanding and insight. Our first goal in studying the parables should be to try to put ourselves in the sandals of those first hearers. If we can put together some of the background of the everyday life in Palestine in Jesus' time, and if we can reconstruct even a few of the details of common life that Jesus drew on for the parables, then we will be in a much better position to share in those flashes of understanding.

For example, modern farmers are often puzzled by the Parable of the Sower, concluding that Jesus knew little about planting. They wonder, *Why does the sower waste so much seed? Why is it tossed on the path or thrown into the thistles?* The charge is that Jesus does not give a true account of a farmer sowing seed. Just a couple bits of information about ancient Palestine turns all this around. In Palestine, sowing preceded plowing. The sower knew that seed thrown on the path or in the patch of thorns would be plowed under along with the rest of the field. There is also a simple explanation for seed on the stony patch: a layer of limestone is very common just below the surface of the ground in that region of the world, and the limestone will show only *after* the plow comes through. So it's not a case of bad farming — but Jesus using the experiences that would be well known to His hearers.

How should we begin to interpret the parables? For some years, it has been widely understood that the parables have one main point. This understanding can be a useful guideline; often the best way to get at the meaning of a parable is to ask the simple question: *What is the single main point that Jesus wanted His hearers — in His time and ours — to understand?* However, it is clear from more recent study that this rule should not be applied arbitrarily. We might do better to ask: *What are the main points that Jesus was making with the story?* It is important, at the same time, to distinguish these points from the extra details included to give the parables their characteristic color and snap.

Is a parable the same as an allegory? Not quite. The main difference is that the allegory is a story in which each detail has a meaning, while the parable has only one or two points. (Augustine provides us with a famous example of what happens when the parables are treated as allegories. In his interpretation of the Parable of the Good Samaritan, Augustine says Adam is the one traveling to Jericho; Jerusalem is the heavenly city of peace; Jericho is the moon, meaning our mortality; and so on until we get to the innkeeper, who is the Apostle Paul. While this interpretation may seem arbitrary and comical, it reminds us to look only for the same meaning that was understood by the first hearers.) An allegory needs to be decoded detail by detail; a parable, though, has a primary point or two of comparison, and the details are provided to make the story memorable and realistic and to support the main point. One additional important difference: the parable is true to life, while the allegory can draw from fantasy. Jesus' stories, being parables, are deeply rooted in the reality of ordinary life in Palestine.

Jesus was a master storyteller. His stories are full of the life that His hearers knew first-hand, full of characters who were both realistic and intriguing. Jesus also uses skills expected of a storyteller which, as we watch for them, will help with interpretation. He employs contrasts, places stress at the end of the narrative, and leads the story toward a climax. As you read the parables, use the same tools and skills of analysis that you would apply to any other story, always remembering that parables were first *spoken*. Ask yourself: *What did the first hearers hear and understand?*

Jesus told the parables in order to draw out a response from His listeners, even to demand a decision. The implied question, at either the beginning or end of many of the parables, is: *How do you respond? What do you think about this story?* And, of course, the decision does not just involve the characters in the story, but is about the urgent call to the kingdom of God and the issues surrounding the kingdom. He who has given us "ears to hear" will not allow us to miss the urgency: We are dealing not with inconsequential stories but with the very reign of God.

# LIVING THE STORY

Choose at least two of these activities for this week.

**Read**     Study John 20:31; 2 Timothy 3:16-17. How does your attitude toward Scripture affect your attitude toward studying parables?

**Write**    List some goals you hope to meet through this study.

**Think**    The parables were spoken by Jesus as a challenge to His listeners. What is your reaction to the possibility that different listeners may come to different conclusions? Is it always possible to have absolute or final answers about all concepts relating to God? If not, what do you do when you face an unanswerable question or a difference of opinion?

**Pray**     Find a ten-minute place in your day to be alone with God. Follow these guidelines for prayer during the week.

**Day 1**    Ask God for an open mind to receive His wisdom as it unfolds in the parables.

**Day 2**    Pray for a new excitement about the value of Scripture in your life as you study and apply it.

*Day 3*    Thank God for the many ways He speaks to people about growing in knowledge of and relationship with His Son.

*Day 4*    Pray for the Holy Spirit's guidance to help you grow spiritually as you submit to God's standards rather than human standards.

*Day 5*    Ask God for opportunities to share the truths and personal applications you learn through this study of the parables.

# OUTSIDERS IN
### *The Great Banquet*

## LEARNING THE STORY

Read Luke 14:15-24. Then read Luke 14:1-14 for the setting of this parable.

1. Describe the setting in which Jesus told the Parable of the Great Banquet, using as many details as you can find in Luke 14.

2. To whom was this parable originally directed? Who are the modern-day Pharisees?

3. Why did the invited guests give excuses rather than attend the banquet? What excuse(s) do you give if there is something you would prefer not to do?

4. If you consider the invitation to the banquet as Christ's invitation to us for salvation, what excuses do you hear from people unwilling to make this commitment?

5. Why did the host become angry? What did he do with his anger?

6. Why does the host send his servant to invite the poor to the banquet?

7. What do "the poor, the crippled, the blind, and the lame" have in common? Why does Jesus describe them so specifically, rather than simply use a general, inclusive term?

8. Why does the servant go out a second time (v. 23) to invite people to the banquet?

9. In verse 21, the servant is instructed to go "into the streets and alleys of the town" while in verse 23 he is to go "to the roads and country lanes." Why the distinction?

10. Are there certain people who should not be included in God's invitation to enter the kingdom? If so, list them.

11. Why did the host think that the servant would have to *make* the last group of guests come in? If you lived in a humble environment and someone invited you to a palace, would you need a little more persuasion to be convinced the invitation was genuine?

12. What does verse 23 tell us about the character of God?

13. Why will none of the initially invited guests taste the banquet? Who made the decision whether they would be in attendance? Could the banquet wait until another time?

14. Those excluded from the banquet excluded themselves. The host invited them, even insisted, but they made the decision to stay away. Describe a situation from your experience in which people separate themselves from God's grace.

15. Why is a banquet a good illustration of what God offers to humankind? What does God offer?

16. When did you begin to identify with the story? Check as many as apply.

___ Having neither the time nor the interest to accept God's invitation of salvation.
___ Recognizing that God's offer cannot wait.
___ Having an increased awareness that God's invitation is open to all.
___ Other_____

17. In a sentence or two, capture the basic truth(s) that Jesus was expressing in this story. Write the truth(s) on page 73, *The Parables Speak to Me.*

18. How would you identify today's poor, crippled, blind, and lame, or those on the "roads and country lanes"? How are they overlooked when we as God's people extend the invitation?

# LOOKING BEHIND THE STORY
Luke 14:15-24

**Setting**
When a prominent Pharisee invited Jesus to a dinner party at his home one Sabbath, He took the opportunity to teach. He first illustrated, with a sharp aside to the assembled guests, how people are more important than religious traditions. His method: healing the man suffering from dropsy (edema). Then, in the course of the table-talk, Jesus proceeded to discuss various aspects of dinner etiquette relating to guests and to the host. Of course, for those with ears to hear, the implications went far beyond mere manners.

This, then, is the setting of the telling of the Parable of the Great Banquet: Jesus at dinner in the house of a leading Pharisee and surrounded by members of that rather stuffy, definitely self-righteous, religious clique.

After a word of advice from Jesus to the host about how he (the host) should go about inviting guests to his next dinner party, one of the other guests says, "Blessed is the man who will eat at the feast in the kingdom of God." It is tempting to think that this guest is feeling a bit uncomfortable for the host and thinks it best to try to change the subject. However, it is more likely that he has actually caught a glimpse of what Jesus is teaching and recognized in Jesus' talk of dinner guests and feasts an image of the kingdom of God.

In Jesus' day, the Jews often thought of the time when God would establish His kingdom in terms of a great banquet. The guest's comment seems to indicate a degree of certainty about his own invitation to the banquet which, he thought, he would accept when it came. Jesus' response must shake him out of his calm complacency, for He says in effect, "The invitation has already come; how will you respond?" In the same way, it calls us out of our malaise of excuse-making and to active response to the invitation of the Gospel.

## Invitation
In the context of Jesus' ministry, the Parable of the Great Banquet stresses the seriousness of His call to repentance and belief. The invitation to the banquet is the urgent invitation to enter the kingdom of God through belief in Jesus. The connection between the guest's comment about eating in the kingdom of God (v. 15) and the parable about the invitation to a banquet and who will actually be able to enjoy it is quite clear. The conclusion (v. 24) is inescapable: Those who refuse the invitation will be excluded; they will have only themselves to blame, for they exclude themselves. The host insists that they come, but they make the decision to decline. No one can enter the kingdom of God without His invitation, and no one remains outside the kingdom except by his or her own choice.

It may have been the usual tradition in Jesus' time to offer a double invitation—one sent in advance and another just before the event was to begin. Members of Jerusalem society expected to be invited twice to a banquet. It is clear in Luke's account of the parable that a formal invitation was sent; then, when everything was finally prepared, a servant went personally to give the message, "Come, for all is now ready." Of course, the irony and the wonder of the story is that these guests are not the ones who enjoy the meal.

19

## Excuses

What about the excuses? They seem rather silly or facetious. Who would buy land without having at least a look at it? Or who would make a major investment in farm animals but risk the ongoing profitability of the enterprise by not first making certain that they are healthy, sturdy beasts? And we hardly need to comment on the third excuse. But are these three really any different from the excuses we make? In the end, these ancient excuses and our modern ones all amount to the same thing: "I think that something else is more important than the invitation to come under the lordship of Christ and to enter His kingdom."

The first two excuses are easily translated into modern terms: "You know, we really have to look after our financial security, especially in these times. You know what the real estate market is like! If we don't take advantage of this opportunity. . . ." Financial security has taken precedence. Somehow, when the invitation to find our present and future security within the family of God comes, we are too busy working on the shaky security of the present markets. "But do you have any idea how much it costs to send a kid to college these days?" we ask. Don't misunderstand; Jesus is not suggesting that we treat our financial affairs irresponsibly. However, underlying all, we hear His words, "Seek first [God's] kingdom" (Matt. 6:33).

In the third excuse, there may be an echo of the Old Testament tradition of a year without responsibilities for newlywed couples. Deuteronomy 24:5 reads: "If a man has recently married, he must not be sent to war or have any other duty laid on him. For one year he is to be free to stay at home and bring happiness to the wife he has married."

Maybe this invitee decided to take advantage of his year off, though it is hard to see how attending a banquet would be too taxing. The third excuse too is easy to translate into modern terms. When was the last time family responsibilities "happened" to enter into an explanation of why you couldn't do something?

## RSVP

Notice that there are two emphases in the parable. We frequently hear only the first part, about the excuses, and then move on to the last line, where those who have refused the invitation are excluded.

Equally important and unmistakable is that *everyone* is included in the invitation. The words of the host, "Bring in the poor, the crippled, the blind, and the lame. . . . Make them come in" (Luke 14:21, 23) indicate Jesus' insistence that everyone be invited, even those usually excluded. Emphatically and simply, the good news of the Gospel is for everyone.

The wonderful wideness of God's grace is thus at the center of the parable. The focus is on the new guests—those who have been unexpectedly invited—and on the host's insistence that his house will be full.

Which emphasis you respond to depends on your perspective. Are you with the first group, too busy with excuses but thinking that you are an insider anyway? Or with the second group: the poor, the disabled, the foreigners—in other words, those who recognize their need of God? Throughout the teachings of Jesus, especially as they are recorded in Luke, those who think they are the chosen ones are, in fact, the ones left out, while the poor and the outsiders are instead entering the kingdom. This parable is great news for the outsiders who are compelled to hear the Gospel and receive the wonderful benefits of the kingdom. But it is a word of warning for those who think they are already on the inside.

Told in response to a comment about feasting in the kingdom of God, this story must have struck its first hearers as saying, "You think the kingdom will come sometime in the future, but that is simply wrong. The invitation to the banquet has come. Now is the time to respond, not with excuses, but with repentance and belief" (see Mark 1:15). Though Jesus directed this parable toward the religious Jewish elite of His time, it is just as relevant for us.

The invitations have arrived. How are you responding? From which of the two perspectives do you view this parable? Are you among the first group, with more important things to do, and so by your own decision excluded from the banquet? Or are you among the second group, recognizing your need of forgiveness and accepting the invitation with awe and delight?

## LIVING THE STORY

David's wife Jane recently invited friends for dinner, but found out a day in advance that the friends' children were ill and so the family would not be able to come. At lunch on the day of the intended meal, Jane mentioned that there would be guests for dinner—a couple and their three children.

"Who are they?" David asked.

"I don't know their names," she replied, "but they have just moved in across the street, and since they are still shuffling boxes, I'm sure they don't have time to prepare a meal. They have just returned from mission work in Peru and must still be in the ordering-out-for-pizza stage."

They had a full house, as planned, though with different guests.

Choose at least two of these activities for this week.

**Read**   Study Matthew 5:3, 6 and Luke 6:20-21. Describe the way these beatitudes relate to the main point of this parable.

**Write**   Compose your own parable using the truth(s) of this parable as your main point(s).

**Think**   Who are the insiders in God's kingdom? Are you one? How do you know? Who are the outsiders in your neighborhood and town? How can you compel these outsiders to become a part of God's banquet? Is it possible to deceive ourselves about our relationship with God in the same way the Pharisees did? What do you think?

**Pray**   Find a ten-minute place in your day to be alone with God. Follow these guidelines for prayer during the week.

**Day 1**   Write a prayer that expresses your response to the Parable of the Great Banquet.

**Day 2**   Pray for a sense of immediacy about sharing the good news of the Gospel.

**Day 3**   Pray for those you know who are not concerned that they are putting off God's invitation.

**Day 4**   Ask God to help you become more aware of those excluded from hearing the Gospel message.

**Day 5**   Pray for ways to reach out to those neglected by the church.

# 3

# VALUE VERSUS COST
*The Treasure and the Pearl*

## LEARNING THE STORY

Read Matthew 13:44-46. Then read Matthew 13:1-43 for the setting and context of this parable.

1. Describe the setting in which Jesus told this parable. Is the setting significant? Who was Jesus' audience?

2. What do you think the treasure could have been? What things considered a "treasure" would not suffer from being stored in the ground?

3. How was the treasure located? What about the pearl?

4. What do the treasure and the pearl have in common?

5. Because the treasure was found, was it free?

6. What about the ethics of hiding something you have found in order to claim it as your own, rather than searching for the rightful owner? Was the finder wrong to bury it again? What was his motive?

7. A dealer in pearls would buy and sell them on a regular basis.

What seemed to be different about the pearl in verse 46?

8. How much time and thought is spent by the finder of the treasure and the merchant in deciding what action to take?

9. What is the most valuable "treasure" you can think of that would tempt you to sell everything in order to buy it?

10. What would "selling everything you have" mean to you? How far would you go—selling your house, your business, your children, your life?

11. What is the kingdom of heaven/God? Many of the parables begin with the phrase, "The kingdom of heaven is like . . ." and then go on with the story, leaving the hearer with an impression connecting the kingdom with the concept contained in the parable. What aspect of the kingdom is brought out in these two parables?

12. How can the kingdom of heaven be unknowingly discovered? Can you stumble onto it?

13. Is entrance into the kingdom of God (i.e., salvation through belief in Jesus Christ) free?

14. Do those who have experienced the kingdom of God have a better understanding of its value? Why? Would someone who lives without the freedom of religion place a higher value on knowing God?

15. What do you consider the cost to you of being a believer in Christ? Is the cost different for different individuals? Why?

**16.** The central theme of these two parables can be stated both positively and negatively, using the same terms in both cases. Try to define these two sides so both can be seen at once.

**17.** When did you begin to identify with the story? Check as many as apply.

___ Wishing that you could find something so valuable you would want to give up everything you had to acquire it.

___ Knowing what you are looking for but not being able to find it.

___ Excited about your new life in Christ, knowing that its value far surpasses any cost.

___ Feeling uncertain about the cost versus the value.

___ Other_____

**18.** In a sentence or two, capture the basic truth(s) that Jesus was expressing in this story. Write the truth(s) on page 73, *The Parables Speak to Me.*

# LOOKING BEHIND THE STORY
## Matthew 13:44-46

These two brief parables about finding something valuable appear to be recorded only in outline. What might they have sounded like when Jesus told them the first time, possibly with more detail? Imagine the interest of his audience in such valuable commodities as treasures and pearls.

### The Kingdom of Heaven Is . . .

The phrase "kingdom of heaven" means exactly the same as "kingdom of God." Matthew uses the first expression, while Mark and Luke use the second. Matthew, with his particular concern to make the Gospel of Jesus Christ known to his Jewish community, followed the tradition of holding the name of God in high regard. So, when referring to the kingdom, he stands a little back from actually using God's name, and uses the respectful phrase "kingdom of heaven."

What is the kingdom of heaven, or the kingdom of God, like? (See Luke 17:20-21.) The "Kingdom Parables" (these and others that describe the kingdom) are an excellent place to start looking for more information.

### Just How Valuable?

Though the main thrust of these two short parables is the same—the overwhelming value of the kingdom—the details provide intriguing shades of interpretation. In the first, the treasure is just stumbled upon. Valuables were often buried in first-century Palestine to avoid their being stolen or taken by force, especially in periods of political unrest. If the one who knew about the treasure were gone, it could remain buried for years. The finder in this parable obviously realizes his good fortune. While he isn't specifically searching for what he finds, he has no question about its value! You can almost picture him looking over his shoulder to be sure that no one notices his burying it again.

The Dead Sea Scrolls were stumbled on much the same way this treasure could have been found. In 1947, at Qumran near the Dead Sea, young men were looking for a wandering goat and one of them threw a stone into a cave to help locate the animal. That stone hit an old pottery vessel which was discovered to contain early manuscripts of Scripture—an unexpected, extremely valuable find.

In the second parable, the kingdom of heaven is like a merchant looking for pearls. He already knows what to look for and is searching because of its high value. Do these differences—a surprise find versus a deliberate search—refer to the many different ways in which people come to faith in Jesus Christ? (Notice the connection with Matthew 20:1-16: some work through the heat of the day, others come only at the end, yet both receive the full day's pay.)

In both parables in this study, the extremely high value of what was found demands immediate action. Without hesitation, the finders take steps to obtain the treasure and the pearl. Likewise, the reign of God in our lives is of immeasurable value; we do whatever is necessary in order to enter His kingdom. Imagine the joy in recognizing the value of your find. The realization of God's total forgiveness brings an excitement that leads to action. Finding the treasure, we eagerly respond.

26

## What Is the Cost?

The value of the kingdom in one's life is incalculable. Through His Son, God is offering us a personal relationship that is not only unavailable elsewhere, but is far beyond comparison. The value is obvious, but what about the other side of the coin—namely, the cost? The two themes are complementary. The cost of being a disciple (which is everything) is indicative of the value of the kingdom (which is beyond all computation). The one seeking or discovering God's kingdom must be willing to risk everything for it.

Verse 44 speaks of a man who comes upon hidden treasure. He wants to buy the field in order to gain the treasure legally. Because the treasure is so valuable, he is willing to give up everything else he has in order to do so. He finds it necessary to cover up the treasure so that no one will find it while he is about the business of securing the title to the property. This process may seem a bit shady at first, but there is no question of impropriety here. In this case, under Jewish law, the finder of the money, jewels, or other valuables would become the lawful owner. So he sells everything he has with joy and anticipation to buy the field and its treasure.

A merchant of fine pearls knows the pearl market. The pearl he found must have been outstanding to require the sale of all he owned to buy it. But he reacts the same as the man finding the treasure. Everything is sold in order to gain the objective, the kingdom of God.

These two parables appear only in Matthew. However, a version of the Parable of the Pearl is also recorded in the so-called gospel of Thomas, an early Christian document containing many sayings of Jesus but virtually no narrative. It was written by an unknown author, possibly as early as the late first century.

> Jesus said: "The Kingdom of the Father is like a merchant who had merchandise and who found a pearl. This merchant was prudent. He got rid of (i.e., sold) the merchandise and bought the one pearl for himself. You also must seek for the treasure which does not perish, which abides where no moth comes near to eat and (where) no worm destroys." (quoted in Robert M. Stein, *An Introduction to the Parables of Jesus*, Philadelphia: Westminster Press, 1981, 99.)

Notice that the emphasis is the same as that in the New Testament. The value of the kingdom of God surpasses all else, and we are to seek such a treasure that will not perish.

27

### The Mystery

Our natural response to the prospect of selling everything in order to obtain the kingdom is to question, "But what about the house—my reputation?" Object as we might, what do mere people like us even *have* that we can sell? What exactly is the cost of discipleship? Isn't this new life in Christ—this life under the reign of God—free?

John Hargreaves, in his book written for Third World theological students, *A Guide to the Parables* (London: SPCK, 1979), puts the matter as simply as possible.

What we pay is our whole life as it is lived apart from God. Another way to express it is to say that we give up our independence; we do this in order to be ruled by God (p. 82).

The kingdom of God has a high personal cost. However, there is no doubt or question that entry into it is free. In the words of Isaiah:

Come, all you who are thirsty, come to the waters; and you who have no money, come, buy and eat! Come, buy wine and milk without money and without cost. (Isa. 55:1)

Jesus, when He was sending out the Twelve, gave clear instructions for them to give without pay because "freely you have received" (Matt. 10:8).

How do we bring this truth together with the "sell everything" of these twin parables? This question is at the center of the mystery of the kingdom; entrance is free and costly. Knowing the value of the treasure you have found, how can you bury it again and go on your way? Its high value calls for a decision. Are you ready to sell all for this free salvation?

# LIVING THE STORY

Jane and David have a three-year-old named Kirk who loves nothing better than playing outside. He has enjoyed this privilege all of his young life because of the climates where his family has lived. He was born in Cameroon and lives now in Fiji; in both places it is never too cold to play outside, though it is often too wet!

When it is time to come inside for supper, Kirk nearly always pitches a fit, not because he is not hungry but because he hates to stop playing. For him, supper is free but costly.

Choose at least two of these activities for this week.

**Read** Study Matthew 6:19-21. Compare the use of the word "treasure" there with its use in the Parable of the Treasure.

**Write** Compose a contemporary parable using the truth of this parable. Make it personal by identifying something of value to you, not necessarily what anyone else would name.

**Think** This parable is focusing on the value of your relationship with God rather than on the cost. Where do you put the focus? If you continually consider the cost of serving Christ, how can you turn this around to emphasize the value?

**Pray** Find a ten-minute place in your day to be alone with God. Follow these guidelines for prayer during the week.

**Day 1** Write a prayer that expresses your response to the Treasure and the Pearl.

**Day 2** Pray for God's wisdom so that you can comprehend the value of His gift to you. Spend some time expressing your appreciation to Him.

**Day 3** Ask God to show you things in your life that you have not been willing to give up as part of the cost of this priceless treasure. Pray for forgiveness and guidance in these areas.

**Day 4** Pray for opportunities to share the news of God's free gift of salvation and peace.

**Day 5** Make a new commitment to God that you will continue to emphasize the high value of your relationship with Him.

# 4

# THE LAST WILL BE FIRST
### The Workers in the Vineyard

## LEARNING THE STORY

Read Matthew 20:1-16. Then read Matthew 19:23-30 for the setting of this parable.

1. Describe the context in which Jesus told the parable. Who was Jesus' audience? What topic led to the story?

2. How many different groups of workers are described? What was the financial agreement for each group?

3. Define the "denarius" in the story according to your family income (one day's income for one adult worker). Mentally go through the story, replacing the word "denarius" with this amount. How does this affect your surprise or frustration?

4. Which group of workers received pay different from the original agreement?

5. What was the attitude of those hired first when they discovered the wages of those hired later?

6. Do you think the first groups of workers would have felt differently if the wages earned had been something intangible, such as peace or joy?

7. The first group hired expected higher wages only after they heard what the last group was being paid. When are you most tempted to judge what is right for you by the standards or expectations of other people?

8. After paying the workers at the end of the day, how does the landowner defend his behavior?

9. Compare Matthew 19:30; 20:8; and 20:16. Do you think this indicates a complete reversal of one's position, or an indication that there is no such thing as position in God's kingdom. Why?

10. Being careful to remember that a parable is not a perfect analogy but gives only a picture and not a specific likeness, identify the various characters in this parable.

11. Have you ever been out of work, or known someone who couldn't find a job for a long time? How does this experience affect how you think about this story?

12. How is justice defined by this parable?

13. When did you begin to identify with the story? Check as many as apply.

____ Being ready and willing to do whatever God asks of you from an early age.
____ Standing around doing nothing but ready to accept God's plan.
____ Watching the way God deals with others, and making decisions based on your observations.
____ Assuming you have earned special blessings because of your faithfulness.

—— Being aware that God has faithfully given you everything He promised when you made a life-changing commitment to live by His standards.

—— Feeling excited that God's commitment to you is much more than you could have initially imagined.

—— Other_____

14. What is the message of this parable for those who have been believers and active in church work for a long time? How do we see ourselves in relation to those who have just come to faith in God, or even to those who are still seeking?

15. In a sentence or two, capture the basic truth(s) that Jesus was expressing in this story. Also write the truth(s) on page 73, *The Parables Speak to Me.*

# LOOKING BEHIND THE STORY
## Matthew 20:1-16

### Interviewed for a Day's Work

Jesus told this parable within the context of tough economic times when many were without work. The relations between landowners and workers would likely be a frequent topic of conversation and easily command the attention of His listeners. The "landowner" would be today's owner of a large farm who is concerned with rainy weather at harvesttime or a crop soon to be overripe. The landowner might also be an office manager hiring temporary employees to assist in meeting a tight deadline.

The landowner approaches the five groups of workers beginning "early in the morning" up to an hour before sunset. The first group is offered, and agrees to, a denarius for the day's work. This was the usual day's wage for a laborer and seems to be satisfactory and fair to the newly employed.

As the day goes on, more workers are interviewed. At the second hiring, the landowner describes the rate of payment as "whatever is right"; and at the third and fourth hirings, he does "the same thing."

However, in the fifth hiring, involving the group who stood around all day doing nothing, there is no mention of an agreement about payment—only the assumption that it will be correct.

It is quite striking that the owner (or the CEO, in today's term) goes out to find the workforce, rather than the business manager, foreman, or steward. The foreman is present in the evening (v. 8) and no doubt spent all day supervising and overseeing the progress of the labor. What does it indicate if we understand the owner to be God?

## Payday

Being paid at the end of each day's work may seem a bit odd to us in the modern world. But the Jewish historian of Jesus' time, Josephus, indicates that workmen were paid when the day's labor was completed, partly out of fear that the money would be stolen in the meantime. "For if any of them did but labor for a single hour, he received his pay immediately" (Josephus, *Antiquities*, 20.220).

The payout is reversed. It would normally have been expected that the payment would begin with those who began first. But the householder turns things around and first pays those who were hired last. The result is a sense of expectation in those who have worked the longest. They understandably then expect to receive more than those who have worked only a short time.

Imagine yourself in the place of those hired first. What are your feelings? You work the entire day, bear the burden of fatigue and the fierce heat, and then find that others who had done only a couple of hours of work during the cool evening are paid the same! As you listen to the disbursing of wages, your hopes for a little extra pay are raised; great is your disappointment when you receive the denarius you agreed to. What happened to "equal pay for equal work"? Where are the "merit increases"?

Is this grumbling justified? Since the terms of the hiring were satisfactory, there is no obvious injustice. It is only as the day's wages for the other workers becomes known that the discontentment grows. The first workers then try to establish their worth by comparing themselves to the others—not at all an appropriate standard.

## Justice

This story might justifiably be called the Parable of the Landowner since each aspect of the story is controlled by his actions: He is the one who calls the workers, determines rates of pay, reverses the usual order of payment, and then gives a series of defenses for his actions. Though the discontented workers may have an important message for us, they are not central to the action (or the interpretation) of the parable.

In the literature of the rabbis there is a very similar parable; however, there is a significant change of focus.

> Unto what was Rabbi bar Hiya like? He was like unto a king who hired many laborers of whom one was more industrious than the others. What did the king do? He called him out and walked up and down with him. In the evening the workmen came to be paid. He gave also a full day's pay to the man he had walked with. When the other workers saw this they complained and said: We have been working hard all day, and this one who only labored two hours receives as much wages as we do? The king answered: It is because this one has done more in two hours than you in a whole day. Likewise R. Abun, although he had studied the Torah only until the age of twenty-eight, he knew it better than scholar or pious man who would have studied until a hundred. (Translated in Robert M. Johnston, "The Study of Rabbinic Parables" in SBL 1976 seminar papers, Missoula, Mont.: Scholars Press, 1976, 346. For other parables of this period, see also Harvey K. McArthur and Robert M. Johnston, *They Also Taught in Parables*, Grand Rapids: Zondervan, 1990.)

The details of the parables are strikingly similar, including the charge that equal pay was given to one who did not work as long. But the response is much different. In the rabbinic parable, the justice is familiar and comfortable: "This one has done more in two hours than you in a whole day." Similarly, it is implied that Rabbi Abun was able to study the Law as much in his 28 years as others in a long life.

Now, notice the justice that is maintained in the parable told by Jesus. Those laborers who complain do so not because they have received less than they agreed to but because they are envious of the good fortune of those who came to the job late in the day. "You have made them equal to us" (v. 12) is the main complaint.

The literal translation of the second part of verse 15 is important here: "Or is your eye evil because I am good?" In other words, "Do you view the world darkly because of my generosity to someone other than you?"

This God loves the person who is faithful throughout the day as well as the one called at the last hour. Jesus does not condemn the Pharisees but warns that a desire to live justly according to the covenant should not lead to an attitude that dictates to the covenant God how mercy and generosity should be shown. The line between following God's will and *deciding what God wills* is always thin and fragile. (John R. Donahue, *The Gospel in Parable*, Philadelphia: Fortress Press, 1988, 83.)

Jesus originally told the parable within the context of the Pharisees' particularly narrow understanding of God's mercy and justice. The Pharisees took delight in outlining God's will, not only for themselves, but also for all around them. It is not hard to feel the uncomfortable cutting edge of this parable: Those of us who think we have complete understanding of God's will, narrowly defined within our own experience, must recognize the wonderful wideness of His mercy which is, in His terms, also justice.

### The Compassionate Employer

Coming to terms with the application of the parable in our own lives begins with putting ourselves in the shoes of the Pharisees and hearing the parable directed at us. Those who had worked all day felt much more deserving than those who had come only at the end of the day. We who think we have God's final word and will on all things too often look down on those in other traditions or think patronizingly of those who have recently come to faith. Even after all of our experience and study of God's Word, are we still reacting from a human perspective rather than God's? God's compassion encompasses so much more than we want to understand. He gives us not what we deserve but what we need. How clearly Jesus' parable speaks to us.

# LIVING THE STORY

Choose at least two of these activities for this week.

**Read**    Study Psalm 139. How can God have this attitude about every person? See also Genesis 1:27; Galatians 3:26-29; and Matthew 7:1-2.

***Write*** Rewrite this story in a skit or drama format in a contemporary setting. Suggestions: Instead of a vineyard, the setting could be a cottage industry which started as a one-person business but grows rapidly until help is needed. Or, instead of a landowner and workers, use parents and their five children. What happens to your parable if the wages are paid in something other than money, such as friendship; or in necessities, such as food or housing?

***Think*** Consider a situation where it would be disastrous if everyone were treated exactly the same, such as giving the same important written directions to a reader and a nonreader. As humans, we have a high sense of fairness. Why do we limit God to our way of thinking? When should we be open to new biblical concepts that may alter our way of thinking? Explain how it is possible to read the Bible yet continue to define God by human definitions. Have you known about God and studied His qualities long enough to know Him very well?

***Pray*** Find a ten-minute place in your day to be alone with God. Follow these guidelines for prayer during the week.

***Day 1*** Write a prayer that expresses your response to the Workers in the Vineyard.

***Day 2*** Pray for an exciting awareness that you can never know all there is to know about God, and for a desire to stay open to new things about Him and His Word.

***Day 3*** Ask God to show you when you are basing your worth on the standards of society around you, rather than on His value of and love for you.

***Day 4*** Talk to God about your desire to see others by His standard, not measuring them by your own preferred style of living and worship.

***Day 5*** Pray for guidance and forgiveness for times when you grumble about the unfairness of a situation.

# 5

# THE WAITING FATHER
## *The Lost Son*

## LEARNING THE STORY

Read Luke 15:11-32. Then read Luke 15:1-10 for the context of this parable.

1. Luke 15:1-2 lists four groups of people who are near Jesus as He tells these parables. Describe each group. What are their differing attitudes about Jesus and His teachings?

2. The parable does not say that the father questions the son's request for his share of the estate. Do you think granting it was as simple and straightforward as it appears? Why does the father grant the request?

3. What does the son do with his share of the estate?

4. What do you think is the younger son's motivation for returning?

5. The father is aware of his son's return while he is still some distance away. How do you explain that?

6. Define "compassion." What situation would cause you to have feelings of compassion?

7. What is the significance of the robe, the ring, and the celebration feast?

8. How does the second half of the parable, which centers on the older son, relate to the first half? Draw out the parallels in details and meaning.

9. Why does the older son react as he does? Is he justified in his attitude? Describe both the emotional reasons and the economic and social problems his returning brother poses.

10. The parable does not tell us the final response of the older brother to his father's words of care. How would you write that part of the parable?

11. When did you begin to identify with the story? Check as many as apply.

   ___ Wanting to escape, even if it means hurting others.
   ___ Dangling at the end of your rope but being unwilling to ask for help.
   ___ Being aware of God's love and mercy but unsure whether He will accept you as you are.
   ___ Standing in complete amazement and awe that God unconditionally loves you.
   ___ Feeling frustrated that you aren't getting any public attention for your faithfulness.
   ___ Other_____

14. Give two or three reasons why this is one of the most widely known sections of Scripture.

**15.** In a sentence or two, write the basic truth(s) that Jesus was expressing in this story. Write the truth(s) on page 73, *The Parables Speak to Me.*

# LOOKING BEHIND THE STORY
## Luke 15:11-32

Few passages in Scripture are more loved than this one. Many of us find the picture of the never-ceasing, ever-available love of our Heavenly Father to be one of the foundational pieces on which our understanding of God's character rests. Yet we're frustrated and indignant at both sons' behavior, even while we identify with their actions and needs.

The request by the younger son at the parable's opening is much more dramatic than it appears. Particularly helpful is the research into the social environment of the parables done by a missionary who has lived in the Middle East for many years, Kenneth Bailey (*Poet and Peasant and Through Peasant Eyes: A Literary-Cultural Approach to the Parables in Luke*, Grand Rapids: Eerdmans, 1983). As there was no custom or law in the Middle East that allowed a son to share the father's wealth while the father was alive, any suggestion that the inheritance be taken early is the same as a wish for the father's death. So the parable begins with an incredible insult against the father. The son declares, in essence, "I cannot wait until you are dead."

Try to translate the difficulty of granting the son's request into modern terms. For instance, your estate will be divided among your children at your death, but to give them their inheritance now would mean selling your home, car, and business. Would you do it?

As striking as the request is, its impact is matched by what follows: the father grants it! In the opinion of the listeners of this story, the father would be expected to react with violence perhaps, and to discipline the son for such impertinence. Instead, he expresses a love deep enough to allow the son's rejection.

Dr. I. Sa'id, an Egyptian writing in Arabic, comments on the parables in Luke 15.

The shepherd in his search for the sheep, and the woman in her search for the coin, (Luke 15:1-10) do not do anything out of the ordinary beyond what anyone in their place would do. But the actions the father takes in the third story are unique, marvelous, divine actions which have not been done by any father in the past. (Quoted in Bailey, 166)

The son quickly sells the property he has gained from his father (he has to leave town quickly due to the consternation of the community) and travels to a foreign place where he runs through his money. Famine strikes and the son becomes an unwanted foreigner without means of support, so in desperation he accepts the job of feeding pigs.

## Coming to Himself

What is the nature of the son's coming to his senses in verse 17? Does he repent? If so, for what? What prompts him? It may well be more than hunger, for he had lost money that was not really his to lose and had failed in his duty to care for his father in old age. But the son might well argue that if he had used the money wisely and not squandered it, he would have no sin of which to repent. So it could be that he is motivated by hunger and sees his need simply to pay back the wasted inheritance. Hardly sufficient.

The son thinks of returning as a hired servant as a means to reestablish himself, which sounds like a good option. The position of a hired servant (one free to live in the local village and earn money) would be very similar to that of the older brother. His social status would be lower than before, but he would be able to earn money and pay back what he had lost. He may have been thinking that he would be able to repay what was actually his father's by right. If so, his thoughts are on "saving himself," and not really on forgiveness at all.

The younger son's return also creates a problem for the older brother, who now owns the farm; the inheritance had been divided between them. According to Jewish custom, the father had the right to use the income of the farm as he wished as long as he lived. This applies to the inheritance given to the younger son as well, which indicates again the amazing generosity the father shows to the younger son. At this point, it is only the older brother's share that is in question. It is understandable that he deeply resents the return of the younger brother because everything spent on him from this point on represents a deduction from his own future wealth. This might be another reason why the younger son thinks it better to return as a hired hand and live in the village.

Since the younger son alienates his people by his original actions, then returns as a total failure, he expects the villagers to greet him with taunts and harassment. The Middle Eastern farmers lived in villages, not in isolated farms; so many are present to witness the return. But what happens? The father *runs* — something a nobleman from an ancient society would never do — to meet the returning prodigal, essentially taking the harassment for him and protecting him through his own acceptance. The father's hug and kiss show so much more reconciliation and forgiveness than the son requests!

### What Is Repentence?
Does the prodigal return with a partial repentance in mind? Is it his intent to ask to be made a hired servant so that he might earn his status and, for that matter, live out from under his father's authority and away from his brother's house? If so, the father's pure forgiveness is that much more significant, as is the son's acceptance. Note that the son does not complete his planned speech in verse 21, asking to be a hired servant. Has he suddenly changed his mind, overwhelmed by his father's love? Given in the face of the scorn of the villagers, the father's love turns the point away from the lost money to the broken relationship. The son really has nothing to offer; working to make repayment is not going to solve anything. He certainly understands that any renewed relationship can only come as a gift from his father. The son ends his speech in the only appropriate way: "I am no longer worthy to be called your son."

The father turns to the servants and instructs them to dress the son. When the son is seen in the father's best robe, the one kept for special ceremonial occasions, all recognize that reconciliation has taken place. The signet ring shows the trust placed in him, and the shoes indicate his freedom. Then the calf is ordered killed and all the village is invited for the feast. The speech expressing the father's joy tells it all.

### The Older Son
The second half of the story, focusing on the older son's reaction to all this, is a stylistic repetition of the first half. And most importantly, the thrust is the same. The father's response to both sons is identical! Even though the older son expresses his anger vehemently and insults his father by his attitude, he is offered the same love and forgiveness. It appears that this first-born is as rebellious as the younger, yet

doesn't want to recognize his own need or the offer of his father.

God's love, as illustrated by the waiting father, goes beyond our comprehension. Yet we are called to experience it. It isn't necessary to live with a poor decision or inappropriate actions. Why are we hesitant to respond to God's obvious desire to forgive us? God responds so generously to our short, stumbling steps toward Him; all we have to do is turn to Him.

# LIVING THE STORY

Choose at least two of these activities for this week.

**Read**   Study Luke 15:3-10. What message do the Parables of the Lost Sheep and of the Lost Coin have in common with the Lost Son?

**Write**   Compose an acrostic with the word "UNCONDITIONAL." For each letter, use a word or phrase that describes God's attitude toward you. Begin with U—Unlimited forgiveness.

**Think**   Which brother represents you and your response to God? Are you like the younger brother, aware that God has forgiven you of much more than is humanly possible? Or do you identify with the older brother, having been faithful to God for years? As the older brother living under the influence of the father all these years, how is it possible to have such a "human," selfish reaction to the position of others?

   As a longtime Christian, do you now automatically have God's attitude of compassion and forgiveness? Why or why not?

**Pray**   Find a ten-minute place in your day to be alone with God. Follow these guidelines for prayer during the week.

**Day 1**   Write a prayer that expresses your response to the Lost Son.

**Day 2**   Ask God to overwhelm you with a sense of His love for you.

*Day 3*   Rather than making your own decisions, pray that the Holy Spirit will open your eyes and ears to become more sensitive to God's direction.

*Day 4*   Ask God for His love and understanding in your family relationships and responsibilities, especially with your brothers and sisters.

*Day 5*   Pray for God's help in showing His unconditional love and acceptance to those who are unaware that it is available to them.

# 6

# ORDINARY SAINT
*The Farmer and the Servant*

## LEARNING THE STORY

Read Luke 17:7-10. Then read Luke 17:1-6 for the context of this parable.

1. Describe the context in which Jesus told this parable. Why is the context significant?

2. If someone repeatedly hurt you and then asked for forgiveness, would you pray, "Lord, this is too much to ask of me"? Or knowing how high God's standards are, would you say, "I can only do it if He will increase my faith"? (See vv. 3-5.)

3. To whom was this parable originally directed?

4. "One of you" is the overseer of the servant. How many servants are there? What kind of relationship exists between the one giving the instructions and the servant?

5. What is the servant requested to do? Are these unusual or difficult tasks? What is the natural response of the servant?

6. Describe the difference between the relationship implied in the parable and the typical employer-employee relationship today?

7. What experience have you had as a servant, or directing the tasks of a servant? How does this experience change your response to this parable?

8. Read verse 10 in several different translations of the Bible. What is your response to the word "unworthy" or "unprofitable"? Do you consider it a demeaning term?

9. What is the meaning of "duty"? Write down your definition, then check the dictionary. Is there a difference? Which meaning applies to this parable?

10. Compare Luke 17:10 to 17:4. Does this fit your definition of duty?

11. The servant works in the fields and now does the cooking and serving as well. How much more does he have to do in order to earn a relationship with the farmer?

12. When in our journey of faith will we be able to earn God's grace?

13. Read Luke 12:35-38 and compare it to this parable in Luke 17. What are the differences and similarities in details as well as in meanings?

14. When did you begin to identify with the story? Check as many as apply.
    ___ Wishing that you could be the one served.
    ___ Being happy to serve and take care of everything.
    ___ Feeling frustrated that you are not equal with the master.
    ___ Being honored that God would ask you to be His servant.
    ___ Recognizing service to God as a normal, everyday part of your relationship with Him.
    ___ Other_____

**15.** In a sentence or two, capture the basic truth(s) that Jesus was expressing in this story. Write the truth(s) on page 73, *The Parables Speak to Me.*

# LOOKING BEHIND THE STORY
## Luke 17:7-10

In Luke's Gospel, Jesus is often the one who serves. In Luke 12:35-38, when the Master returns and finds the servants awake, He will serve them at the table. Then, Jesus places Himself among the disciples as the servant in the important teaching in Luke 22:26-27.

> Instead, the greatest among you should be like the youngest, and the one who rules like the one who serves. For who is greater, the one who is at the table or the one who serves? Is it not the one who is at the table? But I am among you as one who serves.

However, in the Parable of the Farmer and the Servant, the emphasis is turned around, and Jesus is clearly portrayed as the master — the one in authority.

Yet this parable was told at a time when it was unthinkable for a master to serve the servant. Imagine the confusion when Jesus identified himself as one who serves in Luke 12:35-38, to say nothing of His washing the disciples' feet! (John 13) Jesus' teaching about the high value of service is a radical departure from the normal way of doing things. But it is in this context (Jesus as the Servant-Master) that this often-neglected parable is to be interpreted.

### What Is a Servant?
We need a closer look at the master-servant relationship in the ancient Near East, since it is not a common one for us as Westerners. How many of us have even one live-in servant? In the Palestine of Jesus' time and in the Middle East today (as in many other cultures), even the poor have servants in their households. This is often for the good of the servant, perhaps a child from an even poorer family who will at least be fed. In some families, though, a servant may have a high position with a great deal of responsibility for the household and property.

46

The word *servant* is literally translated "slave." However, it was not uncommon for slaves to be given their freedom. The average individual's period of slavery was about seven years, after which freedom was granted. Yet many slaves would remain in the service of the same master because of the relationship that had been established.

Some have argued that this parable was not directed toward the disciples because they would not have had servants. But this argument comes out of the Western thinking about servants. This parable does not describe a wealthy household, for there is only one servant who serves both in the field as plowman or shepherd and in the house as cook. Furthermore, the field may have been rented. And, as is more and more recognized, we have no evidence that the disciples were among the poorest of the poor.

### Not without Honor
For some, being a servant meant having enough food to eat. For others, it was much more, providing security, identity, and meaning. In fact, the benefits for the servant of a nobleman or official in the ancient Middle East were great, making this relationship an appropriate one for Jesus to use in illustrating the disciples' relationship to God.

Yet this benefit does not come from the identity of the servant or even from the tasks done by the servant. No one would suppose that the servant who has done the usual day's chores would expect any particular honor. Actually, the servant in the story isn't being overworked or asked to do anything out of the ordinary. The meal in question is one eaten in the middle-to-late afternoon, not the evening. The servant, therefore, is being asked to prepare something at three or four in the afternoon, not eight in the evening; so there is no question of overtaxing the servant. The master-servant relationship described here is one of authority and obedience, not of inhuman bondage. What happens to our attitude about serving if we solely look at it in terms of the modern workaday world, with employee associations, unions, and carefully determined workweeks?

### Of Course Not
"Would he thank the servant because he did what he was told to do?" This question gets its intended negative response—of course not! But its implication is much stronger than it appears in English. It is not referring to a word of appreciation at the end of a busy day.

Instead, Jesus asks if the servant has any special credit due him. Is the master somehow indebted to the servant who has carried out orders in the usual way? And the answer—of course not.

> The parable . . . warns us against importing into religion that book-keeping mentality which imagines we can run up credit with God by our works. Jesus says it can't be done. So does the Apostle Paul. But the delusion dies very hard. There still survives among us those who think they can establish a claim on God beyond the line of duty. Something of the Pharisee still lurks in their innermost heart. (A.M. Hunter, *The Parables Then and Now*, Philadelphia: Westminster Press, 1971, 84)

### The Master and Lord

Over and over we hear Jesus proclaiming that He eats *with* the disciples and even with sinners, and that He is anxious to come in and eat with us. The disciples are friends and companions, not servants. But throughout these times, Jesus remains in authority; the believer is called to follow His example in service, but Jesus is always the Master. In this parable, He is emphasizing His place as Lord, even to the extent of describing the servant's proper place of putting the Master first and eating *after* He has finished.

Yet do we respond to Christ as the servant or as the Master? Is it the Master serving the slave, or the slave serving the Master? Because we are believers in Jesus, the Son of God, we may think we should have a special place of privilege among God's creation. Is this our motivation to believe and come under submission to Christ?

What *are* our motives in serving Him? Is it in order to gain something, maybe even something we desire for someone else? Or does it come naturally out of the secure relationship we have with our Master? Since it is impossible to have a claim on God, our service cannot earn us that reward. There is nothing that we can do that will put us in God's debt; our service is a normal, ordinary part of our worship.

Paul calls himself a slave, or servant, of Christ in a positive and honorable sense, as the word is used in this parable. As servants of Jesus Christ, we are not simply employees, working set hours and, therefore, expecting set wages as our due. Instead, as disciples, we are as slaves for whom the Master takes complete responsibility, in whose care we live in complete security and trust. Our commitment, our work is done out of loyalty and devotion as part of the normal and accepted relationship. At the end of the day, we can say to the Master, "We have joyfully done our duty."

# LIVING THE STORY

Choose at least two of these activities for this week.

**Read**    Study Proverbs 3:5-6 and Psalm 62:5-8. Are you trusting God to have total control of your life?

**Write**    God gives us everything we need to live, from life-sustaining breath and the ability to experience joy, to the privilege of a personal relationship with Him. Make a list of the necessities and the blessings provided for you by God.

As you look back over your list, what is your attitude toward this giver of life? Do you expect God to thank you for experiencing His joy?

**Think**    Are you living in total submission to the lordship of Christ, or looking to God as the one who serves you by answering all of your prayers?

Do you balance your understanding of the nature of God by viewing Him both as the sovereign Lord and as the one who serves His creation?

**Pray**    Find a ten-minute place in your day to be alone with God. Follow these guidelines for prayer during the week.

**Day 1**    Write a prayer that expresses your response to the Farmer and the Servant.

**Day 2**    Ask God to show you His attitude toward you as a servant and as your Lord.

**Day 3**    Thank God for His qualities that give you peace to be His servant.

*Day 4*   Pray for guidance to have a serving attitude toward people who do not know Christ as Lord.

*Day 5*   Ask God to bring you to a greater understanding of His place of Lord in your life.

# 7

# AS GOD HAS FORGIVEN US
### The Unforgiving Servant

## LEARNING THE STORY

Read Matthew 18:23-35. Then read Matthew 18:21-22 for the setting of this parable.

1. Describe the setting in which Jesus told this parable. Why is the setting significant?

2. To whom was this parable originally directed?

3. List the characters in this parable. What is their relationship to each other?

4. Explain the concept of "settling accounts."

5. If a talent is equal to 15 years wages, what would 10,000 talents equal in today's economy, using your family income as a guide? If a denarius is one day's wage, calculate the value of 100 denarii to your family *today*.

6. Does the first servant ask for the debt to be forgiven? How does the king respond?

7. What do you think would have happened if the servant had

accepted his fate and not asked for mercy? Can you receive God's forgiveness without asking for it?

8. What circumstances convince the king to cancel the debt? What kind of king is willing to simply wipe out a debt of that size?

9. How would you expect the servant to react on hearing the news of this cancellation? What is the normal human reaction to such unexpected news?

10. Read through the parable again and note every parallel detail between the first and second debtors.

11. Why do the other servants react in distress and tell the king what has happened?

12. What standard does the king use when he tells the first servant how he should act?

13. The phrase "from your heart" in verse 35 is one of the keys to the passage. What does it mean?

14. The story is quite graphic, even shocking. What are we to do with the forgiveness we have received from God?

15. When did you begin to identify with the story? Check as many as apply.

____ Being accountable for a debt you cannot pay.
____ Feeling grateful for God's forgiveness.
____ Becoming intolerant of anyone who doesn't measure up to your expectations.

___ Being conscious of the responsibility to forgive others.
___ Seeing injustice and reacting to it.
___ Other_____

**16.** In a sentence or two, capture the basic truth(s) that Jesus was expressing in this story. Write the truth(s) on page 73, *The Parables Speak to Me.*

**17.** How have you responded to God's willingness to cancel your debt of sin and wrongdoing?

## LOOKING BEHIND THE STORY
### Matthew 18:23-35

Peter approaches Jesus and asks how many times he would have to forgive the one who had done him wrong. Thinking himself particularly generous (the rabbis had indicated that three times would be sufficient), Peter suggests as many as seven times. Jesus' answer is well known: "Not seven times, but seventy-seven times"—or even 490 times (see 18:22, NIV text note). That is, it is not appropriate to count toward any quota: there are no limits to forgiveness. Then Jesus tells this parable to explain why forgiveness is to be unlimited. "Therefore . . . "

**How Much Am I Forgiven?**
The sum owed by the servant is unbelievably large; the talent was the largest denomination of currency, and 10,000 was the highest numeral used in Greek arithmetic. The sum was equal to about 50 million denarii; and when we remember that the denarius was one day's wage, we can see the enormity of the debt. In modern terms, this would be something like four or five billion dollars—an impossible personal debt! But Jesus is illustrating the measure of God's forgiveness.

It has been suggested that the details of the story might relate to a treasurer or head of the tax division in the government of an ancient Near Eastern kingdom. The money owed would then represent the taxes due for a particular time period, and the request in verse 26 would be for an extension. But the sum owed may be too large even for this explanation; the tax burden of Galilee and Perea together amounted to only 200 talents, a far cry from the 10,000 owed.

The debtor pleads on his knees and makes the impossible promise to pay back everything. His desperation simply emphasizes the overwhelming load of debt. Then comes the shock — the wonder — of the king's forgiveness. The king does not grant an extension, but simply wipes the debt away.

### How Much Do I Forgive?

The size of the first debt and the king's unexpected forgiveness put the grotesque nature of the servant's refusal to forgive his fellow servant into perspective. The debt forgiven the first servant is 500,000 times greater than the debt owed to him by the second servant. There is hardly a comparison, which makes the lack of forgiveness on the part of the first servant all the more scandalous. And the reason we are to forgive in a limitless manner becomes amazingly clear.

That the other servants are upset is understandable, as is the king's reaction to the unforgiving servant. Notice that the king puts his judgment in the form of a question (v. 33), requiring the servant to face his failure to forgive. And since the servant showed no mercy, he is again in a completely hopeless situation: How can he ever repay the equivalent of four or five billion dollars?

The theme of forgiveness hits us hard enough in Jesus' call to forgive 77 times (v. 22). It may be that the Greek text here should be translated 70 x 7 times; but as soon as we begin quibbling about 77 times, or 70 x 7 times, or any exacting, quantitative approach to forgiveness, we have missed the point. Jesus is teaching about His limitless, qualitative attitude. Knowing this, how much more do we feel the impact of this striking, disquieting story and His final words in verse 35.

Though the king represents God in the parable, there are some details about the king that do not reflect God's character, such as his throwing families in prison for the unpaid debt of one member. Such details are part of the color of the story, but they cannot necessarily be transferred to the character of God.

According to Jewish law, a debtor would be sold only to repay a theft, and in no case would other family members be sold. However, it was common practice in other ancient Near Eastern countries to sell the family to repay a debt (v. 25). It was unusual for a debtor to be put in prison in Palestine (v. 30), but again, it was not uncommon in surrounding countries. Yet notice how exaggerated the details are and how forceful the effect of the story—God's attitude toward forgiveness is clearly represented here. While it is nearly impossible to comprehend such a huge debt, the greatness of the debt is even surpassed by the forgiveness. As the size of the forgiven debt shows the measure of God's forgiveness, our failure to forgive a brother or sister becomes an outrage.

### An Eye for an Eye

The request of the first servant is that the king be patient and grant an extension, though it is clear that the servant can never pay such a huge sum. He seems to be thinking of the traditional approach to justice, where one pays his own debts (even if only eventually). The shock is that the king responds, not by granting the request and allowing a longer time for justice to be met, but in simple mercy.

Then, when the second servant asks for patience, the first continues to seek his old understanding of justice. He has forgotten the mercy he has just experienced. The king's question in verse 33 "Shouldn't you have had mercy . . . just as I had on you?" suggests that the "right" attitude is not strict justice, but the mercy originally shown by the king. The righteousness of God is somehow not related to rights which might be claimed or duties which may be imposed, but to simple mercy.

> God's inconceivable act of mercy, which contradicts all human notions of justice, is so displayed that the listener can only stand in awe and amazement . . . remembering always the great forgiveness of God and extending such forgiveness to others. For when the forgiveness that has been received is not shown to others, it no longer has meaning for the heart and God takes it back. The phrase "with your whole heart," . . . keystones the whole passage, and indeed the New Testament. God's forgiveness is not for decoration but for use. (Eduard Schweizer, *The Good News According to Matthew*, Louisville, Ky.: John Knox Press, 1975, 378–79.)

The Old Testament background for Matthew 18:22 comes from Genesis 4:24, where Lamech proposed vengeance 77 times for any action taken against himself. Jesus turns this around completely, calling not for unlimited vindictiveness but for unlimited forgiveness. Says Schweizer, "The world bearing the stamp of Adam's fall is restored to wholeness through the disciples of Jesus" (*The Good News*, 377).

We are to extend forgiveness with the same measure with which we have been forgiven. God's forgiveness for us is unlimited, even beyond understanding. Yet, as vividly illustrated in this parable, He does expect us to act in a manner that reflects the overwhelming grace shown to us. We have been forgiven; we must show that forgiveness to others.

# LIVING THE STORY

"She just took advantage of me. I think she did it on purpose. Our friendship must not be as special as I thought!" Sally was talking about Connie's rudeness and letting Darlene know all the details.

"When Connie asked if I wanted to go out to lunch, I never dreamed that she just wanted a ride to the restaurant. She actually sat at another table with other friends, and I was left to eat by myself."

"Didn't she apologize or anything?" asked Darlene, trying to ease over Sally's anger.

"Well, sort of, I guess. But I haven't forgiven her. I'm not sure I ever will! Why should I? What she did was nothing short of unforgivable! I couldn't believe she was so mean in the first place. Why should I forgive her? She doesn't deserve it!"

Choose at least two of these activities for this week.

**Read**   Study Matthew 5:7; 6:9-15; and Colossians 3:13. Why is this concept repeated numerous times in Scripture?

**Write**   Make a list of ways (such as putting notes on your calendar) to remind yourself in the months ahead of your huge debt of sin that God has canceled.

   Beside this list, write down the appropriate emotions and responses you have to this forgiveness.

*Think*   What is the most "unforgivable" thing you can think of? Would God forgive someone who does this? Can you? What if you won't?

*Pray*   Find a ten-minute place in your day to be alone with God. Follow these guidelines for prayer during the week.

*Day 1*   Write a prayer that expresses your response to the Unforgiving Servant.

*Day 2*   Pray for God's wisdom to see when you are unforgiving of others and the steps you should take to change.

*Day 3*   Thank God that His forgiveness is available anytime you ask for it, not just at salvation when you are beginning your relationship with Him.

*Day 4*   Ask God to help you to consistently have His attitude of forgiveness. Let this forgiveness extend to those people you don't know, such as the rude motorist, the rowdy neighbor, or the boy who always seems to bully your son.

*Day 5*   Pray the Lord's Prayer from Matthew 6:9-15, and then focus on verse 12. Express this part of the prayer in your own words and ask God to keep challenging you with its message.

# 8

# GUARANTEED INVESTMENT
### *The Talents*

## LEARNING THE STORY

Read Matthew 25:14-30.

1. This parable begins with "Again" (NIV) or "For" (RSV). What does this signify?

2. What were the specific instructions given to the servants? How did they carry them out?

3. Describe the relationship that must exist when a master entrusts his property to servants.

4. If you didn't know the ending of the story, which servant would you think acted properly? Is it possible that the first two took unnecessary risks with someone else's money?

5. If the "talent" in the parable refers to money, what is the meaning of the phrase, "each according to his ability"?

6. On his return, how did the master respond to the first and second servants? How are these responses different? Does this have any implication for our approach to daily life?

7. How does the third servant describe the master? (v. 24) What other details in the story support this opinion? In what way did this attitude affect his behavior?

8. Do you think the third servant acted wrongly? Why does the master react so harshly? Is it really because no interest was made on the capital?

9. What can verse 29 mean? How can something be taken away from the one who has nothing to start with?

10. Is there any sense of justice taught in this parable?

11. Read Matthew 25:1-13. What points do the Parables of the Talents and of the Ten Virgins share?

12. Read the similar parable found in Luke 19:11-27. What are the differences and similarities in details and meanings? Is the main point the same in both?

13. If God has entrusted you with the good news of His love for all persons, how can you invest it?

14. What happens if you hide the facts that you believe Jesus is the Son of God?

15. Obviously, the master was interested in the responsible care of his property. What if the servants had invested the money and lost it? How do you think the master would have responded?

16. Is it possible to "bury" your talents in the church by only using

them there, or is the church the very place God intended them to be used?

17. When did you begin to identify with the story? Check as many as apply.

    ___ Wondering why someone else was given more than you were.
    ___ Looking for the most efficient way to use what you have been given.
    ___ Feeling excited about the master's response to your investment.
    ___ Searching for ways to make up for lost time.
    ___ Lacking the confidence to use what you have been given.
    ___ Other_____

18. In a sentence or two, capture the basic truth(s) that Jesus was expressing in this story. Write the truth(s) on page 73, *The Parables Speak to Me.*

## LOOKING BEHIND THE STORY
### Matthew 25:14-30

The first clue to the meaning of the Parable of the Talents is in its context: it follows the Parable of the Ten Virgins. The first word in verse 14 ("Again" or "For") indicates a close connection between these two parables. While they share the central theme of "being ready," this second parable goes one step further and defines readiness for us. R.T. France explains it this way:

> It is not a matter of passively "waiting," but of responsible activity, producing results which the coming "master" can see and approve. For the period of waiting was not intended to be an empty, meaningless "delay," but a period of opportunity to put to good use the "talents" entrusted to his "slaves." (*The Gospel According to Matthew: An Introduction and Commentary*, Grand Rapids: Eerdmans, 1985, 352)

Faithful service is concerned with responsible action that produces results, not with avoiding mistakes.

## Talents

When Jesus told the parable, He used the word *talent* in its contemporary meaning, that of the largest denomination of currency in use at that time, representing something like 15 years' wages for a laborer.

The Greek word *talanton* has come to English as "talent," and the English meaning is derived, at least in part, from this parable. *Talanton* has nothing to do with the English meaning of "talent" — personal gifts or abilities. However, it is easy to see within the context of this story how this English meaning developed, along with such common phrases as, "You should use all of your God-given talents."

It is possible that the disciples, the first hearers of the parable, viewed the talents as the specific opportunities and responsibilities given to them, rather than with a literal interpretation — and these may include the individual "talents" (in the English sense) that we also have been given. However, if we concentrate on this interpretation, we may miss the main focus of the parable. Our talents and abilities vary a great deal, but we have all been given something of value to invest. We have the truth of the kingdom of God, and Christ's specific instruction to tell others.

## Investing

Relationships between slaves and masters varied widely in Jesus' time. Slaves often rose to responsible positions and had control of large sums of money. Some slaves gained "freedman" status and then continued in a similar work/responsibility relationship with the former master. It would not have been unthinkable for a wealthy landowner to entrust a large sum of money to a slave who served as the business manager. It makes perfect financial sense, within this context, to distribute funds for investment to "each according to his ability." In a similar way, we know that God deals with us as individuals who have different personalities, capabilities, and "talents."

What is your reaction to the various characters in the story? If you're a little more adventurous, you may identify with the first two servants and admire their willingness to take a chance with their capital. Some of us will side with the third, seeing his action as sensibly cautious. (But don't forget the Parable of the Treasure, where the treasure was found by accident!) At this point in the reading of the parable, we can hardly fault any of the three.

The master returns after a long time. Delay also plays a part in the Parable of the Ten Maidens and the Parable of the Unfaithful Servant at the end of Matthew 24. In all three instances, delay is no excuse for being unprepared or caught off guard. Everyone is expected to be ready, anticipating the arrival of the master. On one hand, delay might seem to give more time to be ready, better prepared; but somehow one slacks off when the return takes longer than expected.

He returned to "settle accounts," indicating that the original instructions may have had to do with investing the entrusted funds — that the servants had been given the money with clear directions to invest it for a good return. (The related parable in Luke 19 adds the instruction, "Put this money to work . . . until I come back.") This puts the master's reaction to the cautious approach of the third servant into perspective.

### The Third Servant

If you could read this story without knowing the ending (a problem, since many of us are so familiar with the parables), the treatment of the third servant would come as a shock, maybe even as offensive to the more conservative among us. If you were handed a large sum of money (15 years' wages) and told to keep it against the day of the owner's return, what would you do with it? If you think the third servant is acting wisely and safely, you can imagine him saying proudly that he is now able to produce the talent just as it had been turned over to him. But the master responds very harshly, calls the servant wicked and lazy, and casts him out.

In the uncertain economic times in which Jesus told this parable, many of the first hearers may well have identified with the third servant. So why does the master react so harshly? Look first at the servant's characterization of him. He calls the master "hard." Clearly, he has developed an incorrect understanding of the master, and so, made an incorrect judgement. To entrust a servant with 15 years' wages is scarcely "hard." Besides, why is the servant afraid as indicated in verse 25? Does his refusal to try investing the money result from his fear that he will fail? Or possibly, from his fear of the master?

Compare this servant with the characters in the two Matthew parables already studied. In the Parable of the Unforgiving Servant (18:23-35), the servant continues to act out of an incorrect understanding of justice; he was not able to mirror the mercy he had received. And in the Parable of the Workers in the Vineyard (20:1-16), those who had worked the whole day thought that they knew how the owner should handle his affairs. Here too the workers err in their judgment. In all three cases, the same Greek word is used to describe the servants who misunderstand the master. The Greek word is *ponēros*, which can be translated "evil," "wicked," or "envious" (Matt. 18:32; 20:15; 25:26). It is not for us to judge God, to declare Him right or wrong, hard or generous; but to do the best we can with the opportunities and responsibilities we have been given.

What about the expression "into the darkness, where there will be weeping and gnashing of teeth"? This expression is also found elsewhere in the teachings of Jesus (Matt. 8:12; 13:42, 50). The worthless servant not only failed to invest, but even hid what he had. Is his being thrown out the final condemnation?

**Guarantee**
"Everyone who has will be given more" (v. 29). This line also comes at the end of the related parable in Luke (19:26) as well as in a different setting in each of the first three Gospels: Matthew 13:12; Mark 4:25; Luke 8:18. Is it as simple as our saying, "The rich get richer and the poor get poorer"? Or is it exclusively describing a spiritual response? It is interesting to read in Luke 19:25 the cry of the people standing around ("Sir," they said, "he already has ten!") when the talent is taken from the last servant and given to the first.

The first and second servants were given different amounts to invest and yet each received *exactly* the same commendation. In spite of the different levels of responsibility, there was no variation in the master's response. Each one was given even greater responsibility.

The Master has obviously placed a high value on the talents we are given. Our challenge is to diligently invest our words, time, and abilities in ways that will bring a return for the Master. What a great opportunity, since God guarantees the investments we make in His name.

# LIVING THE STORY

Five-year-old Larry was staying at the Larson home for a few days while his parents, Pastor and Mrs. Darmon were at a conference.

Larry was a charming blond and fit into the family very well for meals and bedtime. Yet the rest of the day, all he was willing to do was sit on the front steps.

"I'll just wait here," he told Ellen every time she came to talk to him.

"Wouldn't you like to do something? We have a tricycle you can ride. Or maybe we could read together, or make cookies."

"No." He was always cheerful but couldn't be persuaded to move or become involved in any activity. "They said I should wait for them here; I know they will come soon."

Choose at least two of these activities for this week.

**Read**    Study Matthew 28:19-20. Were these instructions exclusively for the disciples to whom Jesus spoke? Are these instructions for an exclusive group of people, such as ministers?

**Write**    God invested 100 percent by sending His Son to die for you. He anticipates your response of 100 percent investment so that those around you can also know of His love. Begin a list of the talents and abilities God has given you that are useful to His kingdom.

**Think**    Many people are taught to fear God as a God of judgment, and do not understand Him also as a God of love. How would this limited understanding of His character influence one's obedience?

**Pray**    Find a ten-minute place in your day to be alone with God. Follow these guidelines for prayer during the week.

**Day 1**    Write a prayer that expresses your response to the Talents.

**Day 2**    Pray for God's wisdom to see areas of your life where you are cheerfully, but perhaps too passively, just waiting for Christ's return. What should you do in the meantime?

**Day 3**    Express your thankfulness to God for investing the truth of His salvation in your life. Pray that your joy will spill over to others.

*Day 4*    Pray that you may see the value of God's investment in you from His point of view. What if this investment were wasted?

*Day 5*    Ask God for guidance about investing His truth with the talents He has given you. Who are the people in your life whom God wants you to pray for and befriend?

# 9

# WHY SEND EVEN THE SON?
*The Tenants*

## LEARNING THE STORY

Read Mark 12:1-9. Then read Mark 11:27-33 for the setting of this parable.

1. Describe the setting in which Jesus told this parable. Why is the setting significant?

2. To whom was this parable originally directed?

3. Read Isaiah 5. Is the identity of the vineyard clear? Was Jesus deliberately trying to offend the Jewish leaders?

4. What right did the owner have to collect some of the harvest?

5. This parable is sometimes described as an "allegory-parable," meaning that several of the details have identities that are significant. Identify each of the characters in the story.

6. How many servants were sent to the vineyard? What happened to them? What did they bring back to the master?

7. When it became obvious to the owner that the servants were being injured or killed, why did he keep sending others?

8. What were the owner's expectations when he sent his son?

9. In the ultimate meaning of the story, why does the owner even bother to send his son?

10. Is it possible the son was killed because the tenants didn't realize his true identity? Why?

11. What reasoning allowed the tenant farmers to think that, by murdering the son, they would obtain the land?

12. Describe the people to whom the vineyard will be given. What will the new tenants need to do that the old tenants failed to do?

13. Who does most of the acting in the parable? What does this imply for the whole history of salvation?

14. If "The Waiting Father" is an appropriate alternate title for the parable traditionally known as "The Prodigal Son," suggest a meaningful alternate title for this parable.

15. When did you begin to identify with the story? Check as many as apply.

____ Caring, like the farmers, for someone else's property.
____ Sending a servant to follow instructions, only to see him receive injury in the process.
____ Feeling excited that the son will be able to accomplish what no one else was able to do.
____ Being willing to harm whomever is in the way of what you want.
____ Being sympathetic with the frustration of the owner.
____ Other_____

**16.** In a sentence or two, capture the basic truth(s) that Jesus was expressing in this story. Write the truth(s) on page 73, *The Parables Speak to Me.*

# LOOKING BEHIND THE STORY
## Mark 12:1-9

This is the longest parable in Mark and certainly the most dramatic. The surprising part is that the owner keeps sending messengers. The fruit from the vineyard must be very desirable for the owner to continue to risk his servants. That so many are sent amazes us, and yet the owner still wants a response from the tenants even after rejection and violent treatment of his messengers, even his son.

Jesus tells the story between what we call Palm Sunday and Good Friday. The parable puts into perspective the history of the rejection of Christ, not only by the Jews, but by all of us who fail to believe.

### The Tenants
Isaiah 5:7 forms the background to the parable. (See also Psalm 80; Jeremiah 2; and Hosea 10.)

> The vineyard of the Lord Almighty is the house of Israel, and the men of Judah are the garden of His delight. And He looked for justice, but saw bloodshed; for righteousness, but heard cries of distress. (Isa. 5:7)

Jesus' listeners would have immediately reacted to the vineyard as a symbol for Israel, just as we identify the "Big Apple" as New York City. But even though the vineyard is the symbol for Israel, the parable is clearly directed to all who reject the Son through lack of faith. It is important not to separate ourselves from the characters in the parable, thinking that Jesus was speaking only of the Jews. He speaks to all of us who refuse to recognize the authority of God and His Son. With that in mind, we can more effectively consider the original setting.

God has given His vineyard over to the present tenants, the people of Israel. When the time comes (the word for "time" in verse 2 is *kairos,* meaning God's choice moment, the right season—not simple calendar time), the owner sends servants to pick up some of the fruit that has been harvested. Jesus, implying that the Old Testament prophets were the rejected servants, was again using the familiar evidence in Scripture as the background for this implication.

> The Lord, the God of their fathers, sent word to them through His messengers again and again, because He had pity on His people and on His dwelling place. But they mocked God's messengers, despised His words and scoffed at His prophets until the wrath of the Lord was aroused against His people and there was no remedy. (2 Chron. 36:15-16; also see 1 Kings 18; 2 Chron. 24; and Neh. 9)

The prophets, of course, were not acceptable to the authorities of their day, and were mistreated in every way. They prepared the way for Jesus and received the same rejection that Jesus is about to receive. In the parable, the owner continues to send even more servants, who were also rejected. Finally then, he sends his son.

The thinking of the tenants is difficult, if not impossible, to follow. How can they ever hope to gain the vineyard by murdering the son? The owner is still alive and, as we see in the parable, is quite capable of dealing with the tenants. Their only hope would be to continue to live in the vineyard until the day of judgment descends. Possibly they were relying on the hope that possession would be determined by occupancy, or even that the owner would simply give up after the murder of his son. But aren't we as irrational in our rejection of Christ and His offer of peace?

When Jesus tells His audience of the pointless, unbelievable murder of the owner's son, He asks the final question: "What then will the owner of the vineyard do?" And the obvious answer comes back. In the telling of this story in Matthew 21:33-44, the listeners (presumably the ones against whom Jesus is telling the parable) give the answer. They say that the vineyard will be taken away from the tenants — those who have rejected the son and even killed him — and will be given to others. The implication is clear: The vineyard is to be given to those who will accept the Son. Acceptance of the Son is the critical point on which the story rests. The "others" to whom the vineyard will be given are those who will believe, including tax collectors, prostitutes, and other "sinners."

Who is the main character in this story? Look for the one who does the planting, puts up the wall, prepares the winepress, and builds the tower before renting it out to tenants. Who sends the long line of servants, time after time, and then takes final action? He is the One who demands a response from us.

## The Son

If we come to the parable without knowing the outcome and without presupposing the interpretation, what the owner is really up to is not clear. Obviously, the tenants are scoundrels; they begin by refusing to give the fruit that rightfully belongs to the owner. Eventually, even the murder of the son comes as no surprise. But why does the owner send him? It seems a rather naive move.

A helpful perspective on the parable comes from the viewpoint of the Old Testament prophets who portray God in the pursuit of people. In the records of the prophets, God is long-suffering (Hosea 2; Jer. 3; Ez. 16). The texts of Exodus 34:6 and Nehemiah 9:17 emphasize the same qualities of God, which are typified again in Psalm 86:15: "But you, O Lord, are a compassionate and gracious God, slow to anger, abounding in love and faithfulness."

Though it is difficult to understand his never-ending compassion, the owner continues to send servants to the vineyard. Finally, he sends the only one left to send, his son, hoping he will make the difference. This is the ultimate declaration of God's patience, of His continual desire for communication with men and women. Though we do not deny that the parable was told "against" (Mark 12:12) the "chief priests, teachers of the law, and the elders" (11:27), this is too limiting an interpretation. We are all included in the much wider audience.

The call to conversion presented in this parable—the call to accept the Son who has so often been rejected—is our call also. Are we careless because we know that God is long-suffering, or will we quickly respond out of gratitude and love? In the words of John R. Donahue:

> Jesus thus summons his hearers to a conversion and warns them of the consequences of rejecting God's continual summons. It summons contemporary hearers to think of themselves as the vineyard workers, confronted by a God who continually seeks them but one they can reject. (John R. Donahue, *The Gospel in Parable: Metaphor, Narrative, and Theology in the Synoptic Gospels*, Philadelphia: Fortress Press, 1988, 55)

# LIVING THE STORY

Choose at least two of these activities for this week.

*Read*    Study 2 Corinthians 5:11-21. God has given us the responsibility of telling others about His Son. What steps have you taken to accept this responsibility?

*Write*    Fill in the chart to show how you heard about the Gospel (for instance, through someone's personal witness, the media, an invitation to church). Then record your reactions to the Gospel. How many different ways or times did you hear the Gospel before you accepted it for yourself?

| DIFFERENT WAYS I HEARD THE GOSPEL | MY REACTIONS |
| --- | --- |
| 1. | 1. |
| 2. | 2. |
| 3. | 3. |
| 4. | 4. |
| 5. | 5. |

*Think*    How many times should you share the Gospel with the same individual? If that person isn't interested, what do you do with that relationship? How long should you continue a relationship with an unbeliever?

*Pray*    Find a ten-minute place in your day to be alone with God. Follow these guidelines for prayer during the week.

*Day 1*    Write a prayer that expresses your response to the Tenants.

*Day 2*    Ask God for opportunities to tell others about your relationship with Him.

*Day 3*  Pray for an understanding of the needs of those around you and how you can help meet them.

*Day 4*  Pray for an awareness of ways that you may be rejecting the Son of God.

*Day 5*  Thank God for the power, courage, and ability to do the work He has called you to do.

# THE PARABLES SPEAK TO ME

Summarize the truths of these studies.

*Study 2*

*Study 3*

*Study 4*

*Study 5*

*Study 6*

*Study 7*

*Study 8*

*Study 9*

# INTRODUCTION

## Leading *More Than a Story*

The parables of Jesus are exciting to read and study. They have the ability to challenge us at every stage of life and any level of Christian maturity. As you capture the intensity portrayed in these stories, share it in as many ways as possible.

The parables were originally *spoken*. To emphasize this fact and take advantage of the impact of storytelling, have each parable *told* (as well as read) sometime during the session. You may want to tell the original parable near the beginning of the session and then retell the parable near the end, using details that are relevant to today's culture. Besides retelling the parables, consider adding a delightful visual dimension with skits or reenactments of the parables.

If most or all of the individuals in your group regularly complete the study portions in advance, do not simply go straight through the questions and so duplicate the study already done at home. Instead, select 5–6 questions to discuss which will provide an overview of the content and application. Be sure to also address any specific questions that arose as group members worked through the study.

Learn to be comfortable saying, "I don't know" to somebody's question, if that is the case. The exciting thing about studying Scripture is that we will always have questions. God is so much greater than our minds can comprehend, yet we are challenged to study, question, and ponder great mysteries. Fortunately, the basic truth of the Gospel of Jesus Christ is quite understandable and there are many good sources of information that can help us find answers about it. If participants pose questions which cannot be answered by you or your group, find out first if the questioners have access to reference materials so that they can do research themselves. If not, be sure that you or a volunteer research the question and report back in the next session. An effective study group leader will take each person's question seriously and do whatever follow-up may be necessary.

Extend the reach of your group study by finding and recommending to the members other resources on the topics they are studying.

Choose methods or activities according to the personalities and interests of the group members. Some will prefer primarily discussion in a large group while others will enjoy participating in skits or creative writing. Be sensitive to what contributes to an exciting learning session for *your* group. We learn from each other, so take advantage of your time together to do group activities that cannot be accomplished with self-directed study.

In summary:

1. Prepare to *tell* the parable in its original setting, or have a volunteer do so. Later in the meeting, retell it with contemporary details, using role play or reenactments.
2. Choose 5–6 key discussion questions to focus on. If you learn that few members have been able to work through the study ahead of time, you should discuss a wider range of questions.
3. Find answers during the meeting (or later, if necessary) for questions that members raise after having examined the passage.
4. Locate additional resources to recommend to your group on the topic of the study.
5. Select methods and activities suited to your particular group's personalities.

## More Tips for Leaders

*Preparation*
- Pray for the Holy Spirit's guidance as you prepare, so you will be equipped to lead the lesson and make it applicable. Pray for your participants personally; ask God to help them as they work through the study prior to the session; and pray for the impact of the meeting itself.
- Gather and/or prepare any materials you or the group will need for the meeting.
- Read through the entire lesson and related Scriptures. Answer the questions for yourself.

*The Meeting*
- ❦ Start and end on time.
- ❦ Have group members wear name tags during meetings until they know one another's names.
- ❦ Spend the first 5–15 minutes of the initial meeting introducing yourselves, if this is necessary. Otherwise, spend some time answering an icebreaker question (see samples below). In fact, you may use any good activity to help members get acquainted, interact with each other, or feel that they belong.

*Icebreaker Questions*
Icebreakers help your people become better acquainted over the course of the study. If the group members don't know each other well, choose questions that are general or nonthreatening. As time goes by, questions may become more specific or focused. Reassure the members that they may pass on any question they feel is too personal. Choose from these samples or create your own.

*What do you like to do for fun?*
*What is your favorite season? Dessert? Book?*
*What would be your ideal vacation?*
*What exciting thing happened to you this week?*
*What was the most memorable activity you did with your family when you were a child?*
*Name three things you are thankful for.*
*Imagine that your home is on fire. What three items would you try to take with you as you escaped?*
*If you were granted one wish, what would it be?*
*Name the quality you appreciate most in a friend.*
*What is your pet peeve?*
*What is your greatest hope? Greatest fear?*
*What has been your greatest accomplishment? Greatest disappointment?*

*The Discussion*
In discussion, members should interact not only with you, the group leader, but with one another. Usually you will start the ball rolling by asking a question to which there is more than a single acceptable answer. You are also responsible for keeping the discussion on track because if it gets out of hand and rambles, it loses much of its value.

Here are some guidelines for leading discussion:

- ❦ Maintain a relaxed, informal atmosphere.
- ❦ Encourage everyone to take part, but don't call on people by name unless you are sure they are willing to participate.
- ❦ Give members enough time to reflect and answer a question. If necessary, restate it.
- ❦ If someone is shy, ask that person to answer an opinion question or another nonthreatening question.
- ❦ Acknowledge any contribution, regardless of merit.
- ❦ Don't correct or embarrass a person who gives a wrong answer. Thank the person; then ask, "What do the rest of you think?"
- ❦ If someone monopolizes the discussion, say, "On the next question, let's hear from someone who hasn't spoken yet." Or sit next to the monopolizer to avoid encouraging her with eye contact.
- ❦ If someone goes off on a tangent, wait for the person to draw a breath, then say, "Thanks for those interesting comments. Now let's get back to . . . " and mention the subject under consideration; or ask or restate a question that will bring the discussion back on target.
- ❦ If someone asks a question, allow others in the group to give their answers before you offer yours.
- ❦ Summarize the discussion after the contributions cease and before you move on.
- ❦ Include in your meeting a time for sharing lessons which group members learn in their personal study time, praise items, prayer requests and answers, as well as a time for prayer itself.

# WHAT, WHY, AND HOW

OBJECTIVE: To identify the parables as God's word to us, eliciting a response to their truth.

1. Read Psalm 119:97-112; John 20:31; and 2 Timothy 3:16-17. Discuss the role of the Bible in our lives, as God's Word and as our guidebook; plus the parables as a part of Scripture.
2. Present selected discussion questions according to the steps in the Leader's Guide Introduction on pages 75–78.
3. As time and group interest allow, choose one or two of these activities to help focus on the reasons Jesus used parables.
   a. The questions which follow can be part of a getting-acquainted exercise, depending on how well the participants know each other. Discuss the questions as a large group or in small groups of three to five, according to the total number of participants.
   ❧ *Why does a story hold our attention?*
   ❧ *What was your favorite story when you were a child? Why?*
   ❧ *How can you say it has influenced your life?*
   b. Ask for suggestions from the group of some of the differences that separate our lives from those of the first hearers of Jesus' parables. Then ask for similarities between their lives and ours. As the group names differences and similarities, list them on poster board or shelf paper.
   c. Discuss the group's understanding of the word *parable* and how it may have changed after doing study 1. Separate the participants into two groups, assigning one group the discussion question, "In what ways is a parable a mystery?" and the other group, "Would God hide His truth?" After a few minutes of discussion, have each group present its conclusions to the other group. Then ask: **How do you feel about beginning a study that challenges you not just to think, but to have reactions and responses?**
   d. Discuss the recommended self-study methods to be used for this study, defining and describing the effectiveness of an "inductive study."
4. Have prayer together as a group for your study sessions about the parables and for God's blessing and guidance.

# OUTSIDERS IN

OBJECTIVE: To recognize the urgency of responding to Christ's invitation to salvation; and through prayer, to adopt God's attitude of inviting all people to receive this Good News.

1. Tell the parable in its biblical setting, Luke 14:1-24, so the group participants may experience it as it was originally presented.
2. Present selected discussion questions according to the steps in the Leader's Guide Introduction on pages 75–78.
3. As time and the interest of your group allow, choose one or two of these activities to help focus on the truth of this parable.
   a. Ask for volunteers to act out this parable, using contemporary excuses and "outsiders." Have a master, a servant, three original invitees, and any number of poor, ill, wanderers, and other outsiders. Allow the players to prepare their excuses and identities before presenting the parable to the entire group.
   b. Have the group create a list on a poster board or shelf paper of all the excuses common today for putting off a commitment to Christ. List the excuses down the left side under the heading "Excuses We Hear"; then ask for responses to these excuses and list them down the right side of the chart under the heading "God's Attitude." Finally discuss whether the excuses would be considered valid reasons from God's point of view.

| EXCUSES WE HEAR | GOD'S ATTITUDE |
| --- | --- |

   **c.** Divide the participants into groups of two or three. Give this situation for each to discuss: **"You are giving a party, all the preparations are made, and then at the last minute, as the phone calls keep coming, you discover that your guests are all excusing themselves. Describe the setting and the preparations. Describe your feelings. What would you do?"** After the groups have spent some time discussing their feelings and solutions, ask them to share ideas with the entire group.

   **d.** Have individuals share the parables they wrote as a part of the *Living the Story*.

**4.** Have prayer together as a group after discussing ways to share the urgency for an immediate response to Christ's salvation.

# VALUE VERSUS COST

OBJECTIVE: To place a high value on our personal relationship with God and compare its value with its cost.

1. Tell the parables in Matthew 13:44-46 so the group participants will experience them as originally presented.
2. Present selected discussion questions according to the steps in the Leader's Guide Introduction on pages 75–78.
3. As time and the interest of your group allow, choose one or two of these activities to help focus on the truth of this parable.
   a. Divide the participants into two groups. Have one group make a list of the values of being a Christian, and the other group make a list of the costs of being a Christian. After sufficient discussion time, have each group share its results.
   b. Ask for those who chose to do the "Think" part of the *Living the Story* this week to share their conclusions. Ask: **Where do we, as individuals, put the focus—on the value or the cost?**
   c. Divide the participants into groups of three to five and give each person a blank piece of typing paper. Ask participants to fold the paper into six sections, tear the sections apart, and write a different word in each section representing something of high value to them. Tell each group to combine all the pieces from each of its members and, as a group, prioritize the values to see if they (the members) can possibly agree on the top five. As the groups decide on their five top values, have someone from each group write its choices on a chalkboard, poster board, or strip of shelf paper so all can see the conclusions. After all groups have written their values, ask for a response to this question: **Would you sell everything you have for any of these things? Which ones?**
   d. Have individuals who wrote parables for the "Write" section of *Living the Story* share them with the group.
4. Have prayer together as a group after discussing our need for a renewed focus on the value of our relationship with Christ.

# THE LAST WILL BE FIRST

OBJECTIVE: To understand the difference between the natural, human response and God's way; and to desire to view life from God's perspective and by His standards.

1. Tell the parable in Matthew 20:1-16 so it can be experienced as it was originally presented.
2. Present selected discussion questions according to the steps in the Leader's Guide Introduction on pages 75–78.
3. As time and the interest of your group allow, choose one or two of these activities to help focus on the truth of this parable.
   a. Ask for volunteers to act out this parable. Have a landowner, a foreman, and five groups of employees, with at least two in each group. If your group is small, have only two groups of employees—the first group hired and the last group hired— since the drama is most intense between these two groups. Allow the players a few minutes to prepare themselves before presenting this parable to the others.
   b. Divide the participants into five groups. Have each group choose one of the following statements to discuss (or write each statement on a piece of paper and have each group draw one).
      * *God is more willing to answer the prayers of those who have been Christians for a long time, since they have a long-standing relationship with Him.*
      * *When things are done the same way for a period of years, it usually means they are being done the best way; time has proven their worth.*
      * *It is not possible to think about people the same way God does, since we are not God.*
      * *If things are done a certain way in one's church, it is better to respect the tradition than try to change it.*
      * *The Parable of the Workers in the Vineyard suggests that we abandon the traditional way of doing things.*

      After time for discussion, ask the five groups to present summary statements to the others.
   c. Discuss the issue of fairness. Ask: **Is it possible, necessary, or**

desirable to have one standard for everyone in the world? When are we to be flexible? Should there ever be a double standard?

    d. Ask for volunteers to share their written skits or other ideas from *Living the Story*.

4. Have prayer together as a group, asking for God's help to see others from His perspective, with His compassion and love.

# THE WAITING FATHER

OBJECTIVE: To respond to the unconditional love of God and be challenged to live with an attitude toward others that demonstrates this same love.

1. Tell the parable in Luke 15:11-32.
2. Present selected discussion questions according to the steps in the Leader's Guide Introduction on pages 75–78.
3. As time and the interest of your group allow, choose one or two of these activities to help focus on the truth of this parable.
   a. As a group, make a list of the qualities or characteristics of God the Father. Write any supporting Scripture references beside each quality.
   b. Divide participants into three groups and give each group one of these questions to discuss: **What guidelines can we take from this parable to help us (1) as parents; (2) in peer relationships; (3) in cross-generational relationships?**
   c. Ask for volunteers to form a panel to respond to some or all of the following questions:
      🍃 *Is it possible to pull away from God without realizing it? Give reasons for your answer. If you think it is possible, what could be done about it?*
      🍃 *Is it harder for you to accept behavior which differs from what you approve of, or to forgive unconditionally (without qualification or boundaries)? If a parent, relate this to your child(ren).*
      🍃 *Which son do you identify with, and why?*
   d. Ask for volunteers to contribute some of their ideas and thoughts from *Living the Story.*
4. In groups of two or three, pray that the truth of God's unconditional, continuous, and forgiving love will overwhelm each one.

# ORDINARY SAINT

OBJECTIVE: To be challenged by the lordship of Jesus Christ and to enjoy serving Him.

1. Tell the parable in Luke 17:7-10.
2. Present selected discussion questions according to the steps in the Leader's Guide Introduction on pages 75–78.
3. As time and the interest of your group allow, choose one or two of these activities to help focus on the truth of this parable.
   a. As a group, create a chart that illustrates our servant relationship with Christ. Use Scripture to support wherever possible. Have two columns, with the headings "My attitude as Christ's servant," and "Christ's attitude as my Lord." Fill in each column with suggestions from the group; for example, in column 1 "Obedient" (1 John 5:3); in column 2, "Careful not to allow more temptation than I can withstand" (1 Cor. 10:13).
   b. Discuss the following questions in small groups of about three to five participants:
      ❦ *As women, do we ever hide behind our role as servants, rather than be obedient to the Master?*
      ❦ *When is it hard to be a servant, and when is it too easy? Is it possible for service to be wrong or overdone?*
      ❦ *Can service be worship? How?*
      Then ask for groups to share their conclusions.
   c. Ask: **What are your reactions to Romans 12:1. What is our "spiritual act of worship"?**
   d. Separate the participants into two small groups and give each group one set of questions: **(1) How is it possible to let my understanding of Christ as my brother, joint heir, and friend override the fact that He is first my Lord? Could I unintentionally diminish this part of the relationship? Or, (2) Am I doing God a favor when I give up my old life? What about the notion of God pursuing me until I "give up" and accept Him?**
      Ask the groups to summarize their discussions for each other.
4. Have prayer together as a group after discussing the need for a God-given understanding of Christ as our Lord and what is involved in sincere service to Him.

# AS GOD HAS FORGIVEN US

OBJECTIVE: To appreciate God's concern that forgiveness be given in the same measure it is received, and to be more aware of the mercy He has shown by offering us unlimited forgiveness.

1. Tell the parable in its biblical setting, Matthew 18:21-35.
2. Present selected discussion questions according to the steps in the Leader's Guide Introduction on pages 75–78.
3. As time and the interest of your group allow, choose one or two of these activities to help focus on the truth of this parable.
   a. Ask for volunteers to act out this parable. You'll need a king, a first servant, a second servant, a jailer, and several fellow servants. Give this group a few minutes to plan their actions and words. Encourage them to role play, using contemporary language, comparable debts, and so on.
   b. Distribute note cards to the participants. After explaining that this activity will be done anonymously, ask them to write down two things that are hard for them to forgive. Collect the cards and have someone write these things on the left side of a chalkboard or poster board under the heading "How can I forgive this?" On the top of the right side, write the heading "How will God help me forgive this?" Take each item on the left one by one and discuss how God not only forgives but helps us to forgive when it is difficult to do so. Jot down short summaries under the second heading.
   c. Divide the participants into two groups. Ask the first group to discuss this question: **What do you do when you have asked someone for forgiveness but the person refuses to forgive you?** This group should be ready to give its recommendations to the other group. Have the second group discuss the situation at the beginning of *Living the Story* and share some suggestions for Sally and Connie with the first group.
   d. Ask for volunteers to share their ideas and thoughts from *Living the Story*.
4. Have prayer as a group after discussing our human need: to be continually reminded of the availability of God's forgiveness and our responsibility to extend that forgiveness to those around us.

# GUARANTEED INVESTMENT

OBJECTIVE: To understand that faithful service to Christ requires responsible activity.

1. Tell this parable in its biblical setting, Matthew 25:1-30.
2. Present selected discussion questions according to the steps in the Leader's Guide Introduction on pages 75–78.
3. As time and the interest of your group allow, choose one or two of these activities to help focus on the truth of this parable.
   a. As a group, brainstorm different ways that God uses people for His glory. List as many talents, abilities, and methods of sharing the Gospel as possible on a poster board or shelf paper.
   b. Distribute note cards to the participants. Ask them to write one of the following statements on their cards.
      ❦ *I don't know how God wants to use me.*
      ❦ *I think I know how God would use me, but I'm not doing anything in that area right now.*
      ❦ *I know how God can use me and I am actively doing all I can.*
      ❦ *I would like to serve God in new, creative ways.*
      Then have the participants discuss how they might talk to someone who makes one of those statements.
   c. Discuss Bible characters that actively and effectively used all that God had given them; then name some who were not very effective. What can we learn from each?
   d. Divide participants into groups of about three to five to discuss this question: **How can I share my faith if my knowledge of the Bible is limited?** After a short time, have groups pool their ideas.
4. Have participants pair up and pray for each other to accept the challenge to invest God's Word in others.

# WHY SEND EVEN THE SON?

OBJECTIVE: To call all to faith in Jesus Christ and to actively share with others the Good News of salvation.

1. Tell the parable in its biblical setting, Mark 11:27–12:9 so the group participants may experience it as it was originally presented.
2. Present selected discussion questions according to the steps in the Leader's Guide Introduction on pages 75–78.
3. As time and the interest of your group allow, choose one or two of these activities to help focus on the truth of this parable.
   a. Ask for volunteers to act out this parable. You'll need a vineyard owner, tenant(s), four or more servants, a son, and some listeners. Allow the players some time to plan their actions and words. Encourage them to role play with contemporary language and setting.
   b. Discuss our responsibility for those who have not come to faith in Jesus Christ. Make a list of all the ways we can express our faith to others.
   c. Ask for volunteers to contribute some of their ideas from *Living the Story*.
   d. Go over the summary page, *The Parables Speak to Me*, reviewing and comparing the truths articulated by the participants. Discuss ways the participants were challenged to think about their relationship with God and what they can do following this study to continue giving this relationship first priority.
4. Have prayer together as a group for any in your acquaintance who know about Jesus Christ, but have made a conscious decision not to believe in Him or accept His salvation. Pray too that the truths of these parables will continue to draw a response in the lives of group members.